STRAIGHT A
LEADERSHIP

ALIGNMENT
ACTION
ACCOUNTABILITY

WALL STREET JOURNAL BESTSELLING AUTHOR
QUINT STUDER

Published by:
Fire Starter Publishing
913 Gulf Breeze Parkway, Suite 6
Gulf Breeze, FL 32561
Phone: 850-934-1099
Fax: 850-934-1384
www.firestarterpublishing.com

ISBN: 978-0-9840794-1-4

Library of Congress Control Number: 2009940177

Printed in the United States of America

To the Fire Starters who each day sacrifice so much so we can be assured that in our time of need great healthcare is available. To those many leaders who invite Studer Group into their organizations, enabling us to fulfill our mission to make healthcare a better place for patients to receive care, employees to work, and physicians to practice medicine.

TABLE OF CONTENTS

ACKNOWLEDGMENTS

I would like to say thank you:

To: Clarian Health Care, Indianapolis, Indiana, and St. Luke's Episcopal Health System, Houston, Texas, the early "laboratories" for the survey that became the foundation of this book. Dan and Dave, you continue to be first movers.

To: The countless organizations that each week allowed additional data to be collected so the survey could be refined.

To: All the healthcare leaders who have been inducted into the Studer Group Hall of Fame over the years...

2009 Inductees
- W. Stuart Smith, Vice President, Clinical Operations and Executive Director, Medical University of South Carolina (Charleston, SC)

- Janet Wagner, Chief Administrative Officer, Sutter Davis Hospital (Davis, CA)

- Martin Padgett, President and CEO, Clark Memorial Hospital (Jeffersonville, IN)

- David S. Fox, President, Advocate Good Samaritan Hospital (Downers Grove, IL)

2008 Inductees
- Audrey Meyers, President and CEO, Valley Health System (Ridgewood, NJ)

- Roddey E. Gettys, III, COO and Executive Vice President, Palmetto Health Baptist Easley (Easley, SC)

- Steven J. Simonin, CEO, Wright Medical Center (Clarion, IA)

2007 Inductee
- Frank V. Sacco, CEO, Memorial Healthcare System (Hollywood, FL)

2006 Inductees
- Christy Stephenson, Former CEO, RobertWood Johnson University Hospital (Hamilton, NJ)

- Tom Wright, COO, Delnor Community Hospital (Geneva, IL)

2005 Inductees
- Charles S. Lauer, Former Publisher, Modern Healthcare (Chicago, IL)

- Gail Boylan, Former CNO, Studer Group (Gulf Breeze, FL)

2004 Inductee
- Clay Sherman, Chairman, Management House, Inc. (Carefree, AZ)

...Thank you for being role models in leadership.

To: Jim, JP, Ben, and Maddie Stanzell who supported their wife and mom as she spent countless hours over these past 10 years creating thousands of slides and making hundreds of phone calls to organizations in which I spoke.

To: Margaret Stanzell, an early Fire Starter and one of the original SGers, who first visited Holy Cross Hospital in Chicago, IL, in 1995 and has been committed to excellence from birth. By working on the assessment survey, connecting tools to parts of *Straight A Leadership*, reading each chapter over and over, and holding to an unwavering belief that I can be better and so can healthcare, you've made a difference. With this book you were there from word one.

To: Rick Outzen who read the first transcription of this book and gave its first shape, and to Lisa Conway, who transcribed those early tapes.

To: Dottie DeHart and staff at DeHart & Company for your daily work on *Straight A Leadership*. Your editing, clarification, questions, and rewriting are appreciated. Also, thank you for your work on the book *Results That Last*, for writing lots of press releases over the years, and for the many opportunities to carry the message to the media.

To: Bekki Kennedy...Wow, what a 2009! You oversaw the production of the books *Leadership and Medicine, Inspired Nurse, Eat THAT Cookie!, Excellence in the Emergency Department, How to Lead Teachers to Become Great, Hardwiring Flow, The Nurse Leader Handbook*, and *Straight A Leadership*—and you also gave birth on October 12 to a new baby boy. Your unwavering focus on bringing each book's message to the industry makes healthcare better.

To: The friends of Bill W., who continue to be my best teachers.

To: My wife, Rishy, for your patience as I go up and down, up and down, up and down, in this roller coaster of life while you stay grounded to home and family. Thank you.

To: My colleagues at Studer Group. We laugh together, cry together, learn together, and share the goal of making healthcare better.

To: All the difference making organizations and people who have been and are part of my life. Thank you for allowing me to share this journey with you. I owe you.

HOW TO GET THE MOST FROM THIS BOOK

Excellent leaders seem to approach their work with a mixture of long-term optimism and short-term realism. They are positive about improving performance and finding practical solutions as unexpected events take place. They believe in the work being done and have a built-in belief that things will be okay.

Excellent leaders are also able to move quickly from long-term optimism to short-term realism. *Very* quickly. If healthcare leaders were pilots, they would be those who could go from 38,000 feet to landing in a short time.

The ability to see things long-term, yet zero in and quickly move details, is a must-have trait in leaders. This trait creates occasions when leaders are told to slow down. They get push back and are even told to be careful for the facts can discourage people.

Facts are facts, of course. It is what is done with them that counts. Excellent leaders understand that the external environment is not going to slow down, so the answer is to build an organization that can move quickly.

No one can be harder on Studer Group than I am. In meetings when we're discussing what we can do better, I sometimes see people around the table slump a bit as the "opportunities for improvement" list gets longer. We need to be hard on ourselves. If we are not, then who will be? Who should know us better than us?

In healthcare, the patient who brings the complaint to someone to be addressed is bringing us a rare gift. The patient is helping us recover trust. The reality is that most of the time patients won't say anything to the hospital staff. They simply leave, tell ten people in the community about their experience, and choose another provider next time. The same happens with staff members: They just leave. Physicians move patients to other facilities or figure out ways to provide more care in their office settings.

The point is that we need to hold ourselves to higher and higher standards. No one else will do it for us. We need to constantly look for ways to improve. As you are reading this book, here are some quick tips to keep in mind:

Relate, don't compare. There are many ways to segment ourselves: small versus large, city versus rural, stand alone versus system, union versus non-union, hospital versus medical office, and so forth. Yet, while each organization has its own characteristics, we are so much more alike than different.

Be comfortable being uncomfortable. The exercises in this book *will* create some discomfort. That is fine. Recently, when I was working with a healthcare system, the CEO gave a 30-minute talk on the positive movement in every metric and kept saying how great the organization was. When I spoke, I cautioned the audience not to feel too great—after all, progress is not the same as great outcomes.

It is good that the metrics in quality, turnover, and financial services are moving in the right direction. But don't call them great. Yes, progress is positive and should be celebrated, but the outcomes are now average. According to noted author and Harvard Business School Professor John Kotter, declaring victory too soon is a key reason cultural transformation fails.

Be hard on yourself. C-Suite leaders and department leaders must be able to see the gap between current and needed performance. If someone else sees it more clearly, there is a bigger issue than the gap.

Studer Group sponsors the National Quality Forum's Quality Award, which is given to one organization each year to recognize its high clinical quality. The past two winners have been Baylor Health Care System, Dallas, Texas, and Memorial Hermann Healthcare in Houston, Texas. In listening to both organizations' CEOs, I've found that they take great care to list the areas that need improvement. In my experience, it is typical for leaders of high performing organizations to focus on what they can do and need to do better.

Connect the dots on opportunities for improvement. If there were no opportunities for improvement, healthcare organizations would have nowhere to go but down. We know that external events, regulations, and a host of other factors negatively impact healthcare operations. So if an organization is performing at peak and something happens—such as less reimbursement, for instance—then the only way to go is toward worse performance.

Most organizations will experience bad months, bad quarters, and a bad year or two, but the better-led organizations will be aware of what it takes to move performance back up—and they will do it. As you will read in this book, high performers move the actions to achieve the goals; others lower the goals to meet the actions.

Mandatory is okay. (In fact, many times it's necessary.) Hand washing is mandatory in healthcare. So are proper cleaning, instrument sterilization, giving the correct medication, using parking decals, wearing name badges, and a host of other things. Why? Because everyone doing the same thing in the same way leads to consistency and effectiveness across the organization.

Yet, when it comes to meeting management, staff selection, evaluation methods, leader training, staff communications, accountability, and other critical issues, methods for doing them tend to be optional. Why? One reason could be that leaders become leaders because they like autonomy. And while autonomy has some advantages, it is crucial for organizations to define what is mandatory, what is optional, and why. When evidence shows a certain way of doing things is the most effective way, that way needs to become mandatory.

Set high goals. I spoke at an organization nationally known for clinical excellence, growth in facilities, and solid financial results. In each area the CEO had set high goals and exhibited laser-like focus. In patient satisfaction the organization hovered around the 50th percentile. Its goal was the 60th percentile.

I brought up to the CEO that in areas where high goals had been set, the organization achieved them. The only area missed was the one with the lowest goal. Why? Because a low goal tells the team the leader is not confident the goal can be achieved. It also creates the notion it is not as important as the areas that have higher goals. It does not create the need to change behavior very much (and of course when behavior stays the same, results stay the same—or get worse). A low goal enables a lack of urgency.

Celebrate the learnings. The assessment and the exercises in this book may lead to your learning something about yourself that may seem negative. For instance, there may be a gap in how leaders see the environment or inconsistency may be worse than you had thought. You may discover more performance issues than you'd realized existed. It might turn out that members of the senior team are not fully on board, the team is not achieving excellence, communication could be better, and so forth.

If this is the case, don't get down. Celebrate the learnings. If we are unaware that something is wrong, we cannot fix it. Cancers that seem to kill quickly are often those that are hard to identify; thus, when they are diagnosed, there is usually not much time left. This book is meant to help organizations get an early diagnosis so treatment can be more successful. Enjoy the fact that you are aware of any issues and committed to becoming the best leader and organization you can be.

Remember rule #62. Years ago there was an organization that was doing well. The central office received a letter from the head of a new chapter who was very excited about what the organization stood for. He had created 61 rules to make sure his chapter was the very best. The people at the central office had never seen such an exhaustive list and complex set of rules. They waited to see what would happen. Several months later, they received a note from the rule writer stating that things had not gone very well. In fact, his chapter had darn near failed. He then let them know he had added a new rule— rule #62: *Don't take yourself too seriously*.

Yes, we are in a serious industry in serious times. However, we are also in a vocation that allows us to work with wonderful people who are anxious to do their best— people who are lifelong leaders and who want to believe in their organizations and their leadership. I am confident that you are or can be that leader and that organization that make a difference. Take time to be grateful, for it is difficult to feel gratitude and unhappiness at the same time.

I am grateful that we are on this journey together— the journey to make healthcare better.

In service,
Quint Studer

INTRODUCTION

The chaotic state of today's external environment is not temporary. For the long term, a key to an organization's success is its ability to adapt to a changing external environment.

We in healthcare are certainly no strangers to change. Over the years in healthcare we've dealt with changing payment systems, the transition from inpatient to outpatient procedures, the rise of managed care, various process-improvement and re-engineering initiatives, nurse shortages (and surpluses), vertical integration, and a host of adjustments.

The changes in the external environment are coming faster and faster. They're more severe. And they're impacting healthcare organizations in deeper, broader, more radical ways.

The increased financial pressures that impact virtually every sector of the United States *also* cause tremendous stress on healthcare systems.

One point of pain? Margins. Healthcare organizations—whether for-profit or not-for-profit (or stock or not for stock)—have always depended on margins. We've always needed for revenue to exceed expenses so we could pay for new technologies, new equipment and new buildings and to recruit and retain a talented staff. If we're to continue to improve patient care, the right tools, systems, and people are critical.

But because most organizations' margins have historically been thin, we've also come to depend on capital sources *outside* of operations. That money came from investment income, philanthropic donations, and a bond market that would provide access to capital with favorable financial rates.

You'll notice I've switched to past tense. That's because the global financial collapse changed the game—for good. Suddenly, organizations not only could *not* depend on investment income, but they found themselves facing a devastating ripple effect. Because investment income was connected to cash, organizations could no longer access capital as they once could. And because organizations no longer had the cash they had once enjoyed, interest earnings declined dramatically.

To add to the problem, because hospital donors were also hit by the financial meltdown, philanthropy took a nosedive. Hospitals that once received significant amounts suddenly found themselves afraid to even ask for donations. I can't tell you how many foundations across the country have said to me, "We're not even asking for any money right now. We're just contacting donors to see how they're doing and make sure they're okay—we're building up those relationships."

Consequently, many organizations have cancelled or at least delayed their building programs. Others find themselves unable to move into newly constructed buildings because of the debt they've acquired and the lack of capital to see them through until the new division could start producing operation margins.

As all of this change rapidly unfolds around us, CEOs and senior leaders around the country continue to do what has always been done: create the best possible plan to deal with the changing external environment. And through various means of communication, we've tried to let managers, physicians, and staff know what's happening in the external environment and what to do about it.

As I've traveled the country over the past several years, I've discovered that the problem often doesn't lie in what organizations are doing; it lies in how quickly they're doing it. The challenge, which gets tougher and tougher, is to move the internal operations as quickly as they need to in order to respond to the external environment and keep the organization healthy. It's not about the plan— it's about the ability to execute the plan.

An organization that makes the "Top 100" list this year or wins a national award or even earns the Malcolm Baldrige Award for Quality cannot count on holding onto its success. The external environment is moving so quickly and margins are so thin that just the slightest change can cause a previously healthy organization to fall into crisis mode. It can happen just like that.

Ideally, an organization will anticipate changes in the external environment and move proactively to deal with them. If that's not possible, be able to move very quickly to address them after the fact.

Through our work with many organizations, we have been able to see how well leaders cascade information about the external environment from the senior C-Suite on down. And here's what we've discovered: *If everyone in the organization doesn't truly understand the behavior that's needed to be successful, the organization won't achieve its goals.* It brings to mind the adage "We're only as strong as our weakest link."

Besides the gap that exists between the C-Suite and the various layers of an organization regarding the external environment, there is another challenge. *Consistency.* The assessment reveals that healthcare organizations are consistently inconsistent. That leads to uneven results and blocks the unified collaboration and coordination of movement that allows for efficient operations.

Yes, many healthcare organizations are embracing the "best practices" that lead to success. And that's good news. But they are also revealing a troubling inability to move those best practices throughout the hierarchy quickly enough to survive in a tough and ever-changing external environment.

Oh, certain leaders can adopt those best practices and get great results. That's why they become "heroes" inside an organization. But today we can't afford to have one or two or even a handful of high-performing leaders. We need *all* leaders to turn in a winning performance.

Everyone needs to achieve department goals. And everyone needs to be on the same page.

This, of course, speaks to the first "A" of Straight A Leadership. *Alignment.*

All senior leaders need to be aligned. And all leaders *under* the senior leaders need to be aligned. Why? Because when even one leader is out of sync with the organization's goals, his or her actions will cascade downward throughout the hierarchy, potentially sending thousands of people off course. The higher up in the organization the mis-alignment is, the worse the destruction.

Action is the second "A." How well are people doing their jobs? Studer Group's assessment reveals how leaders deal with performance issues. It typically shows that 40 to 60 percent of the employees whom managers say are not meeting performance expectations a) don't have the shortcomings documented and b) are not in any type of performance counseling. In effect, leaders are telling 40 to 60 percent of their low performers, "It's okay." What we permit, we promote.

Leaders need to deal with low performers, move middle performers up, and reward high performers.

The third "A" is *Accountability.* When I ask organizations if it's possible for someone to perform poorly and still get a good evaluation, the answer is usually a resounding *yes.* Sometimes, I see such vigorous nodding that I feel like I'm in a room full of bobble-heads!

Organizations *must* make sure people are held accountable—particularly in the area of leader evaluations.

And while most do have a Standards of Behavior contract in place, it's clear they aren't truly holding people accountable for following it. If they were, they would be higher-performing organizations.

I've learned so much by asking these questions. First, just doing the assessment at all is valuable because it helps leaders recognize the knowledge gap that exists between them and the rest of the organization regarding the external environment. That, of course, is the first step toward bridging it.

Second, I've discovered that responding to the external environment *doesn't* require scrapping everything you're doing and starting over. That's the really great news. It's not about new things. Most of the work is adjusting some of the things you're currently doing.

This book explains how to integrate information about the external environment into daily operational tactics such as employee forums and rounding for outcomes. If you're already using these "practices," adjusting them to educate employees on today's financial realities becomes just the next, natural, organic step.

I have worked with some of the country's finest healthcare leaders and feel the same pain that we all feel regarding the tremendous external changes taking place. That pain is tempered only by the determination and perseverance that defines the people who work in this industry.

From the very beginning, healthcare leaders and healthcare organizations of all sizes and all types have shown a remarkable ability to adapt. The difference between the past and the present is that from this point onward the adaptation must come much quicker and must go much broader and deeper than ever before. And I believe it will.

It is my hope that *Straight A Leadership* will help leaders better diagnose the scope of the problem faced, and will provide practical, useable solutions to implement. That way, we won't have to worry about scrambling to catch up to the external environment. We can actually start getting ahead of it—and controlling our own destiny.

SECTION ONE:

THE STRAIGHT A DIAGNOSIS

Before a healthcare organization can get to where it's going, its leaders must understand where they are today. In this first section of *Straight A Leadership*, we'll walk you through a 16-question assessment that Studer Group gives new clients.

This assessment sheds light on how critical it is that all leaders view the changing external environment—and the specific challenges it creates—in the same way. It will also help you:

- Understand your own "big picture" in terms of what you do well (and not so well)
- Properly train leaders to *be* leaders
- Deal with performance issues
- Hold leaders accountable for meeting their goals
- Implement and standardize best practices throughout the organization
- Keep in mind how patients, families, and physicians rate your organization

This section explores why Alignment, Action, and Accountability are so important to creating an organization that can adapt to meet the demands of a changing external environment—and become a better place for patients to receive care, employees to work, and physicians to practice medicine.

CHAPTER ONE:

ALIGNMENT

These are turbulent times. We in healthcare have always had turbulent times. When people are asked at Studer Group conferences if their plates are full, all of the hands go up. "If I had asked you that same question ten years ago, would your plate have been full then, too?" All of the hands go back up.

When asked what the difference is between today and maybe 10, 15, or 20 years ago, most people answer, "I did not know what a full plate was back then, but I do now."

It's true. The massive economic forces that have buffeted our industry and America as a whole have put great pressure on healthcare professionals. As a group, we've proven over the years that we can adapt, but the changes happen much faster and go much deeper these days. We must perpetually do more with less.

Our experience tells us that successful organizations are able to quickly make *internal* changes to best meet the challenges of the *external* ones—and that those changes can achieve their desired outcome only if everyone is on the same page.

It comes down to three key components: **A**lignment of capital (human and non-human), taking the correct **A**ctions, and the ability to hold people **A**ccountable. These are the Three "A"s of Leadership.

Gone are the days when a couple of executives can sit around a table and brainstorm quick fixes to respond to the changing external environment. No longer can we take a few hours out of nursing, delay a capital project, fast track a new outpatient procedure, or buy a new piece of technology to overcome these external changes and avoid operating margin decreases.

Success Depends on Better Execution.

While there are still some changes that can be made by a few people and generate a positive impact, the reality today is that success depends on better execution across the board. To handle decreases in reimbursement, investment income ups and downs, philanthropic giving, and the challenge of borrowing money at affordable rates, healthcare providers must increase their performance and thus improve execution.

A big part of execution involves leaders listening and then sending a clear message, and others hearing it, followed by action. The message must help stakeholders understand exactly what is happening in the external environment. It must convey what can be done internally to offset the impact of changes in the external environment.

And it must call on all to offer ideas on what can be done to improve operational performance.

> All sectors of an organization need to be in alignment so that everyone will act in a coordinated and collaborative fashion throughout the organization. A shared sense of urgency must cascade over all levels. What will separate the winners and the losers in these times will be the ability to quickly execute the correct actions.

Diagnose, Then Treat.

A physician diagnoses a patient prior to creating a treatment plan. That diagnosis is a combination of acquired knowledge and experience, and usually includes tests to gauge the condition of the patient. At Studer Group, we diagnose an organization in order to design an effective treatment plan—rather than rushing into treatment based simply on the latest buzzword, the latest fad, or the latest bestselling book.

Our organization pioneered Evidence-Based Leadership℠ (EBL) in healthcare. The concept has its roots in the practice of medicine. Turbulent times and accelerated change made it harder for physicians to achieve the best outcomes for their patients, so they responded by developing evidence-based medicine. In summary, physicians were seeing too much variation in the clinical treatment of patients, and research clearly demonstrated that consistent practice patterns and methods could improve care. So standard treatment practices were created based on the evidence provided by that research.

Evidence-Based Leadership takes the same approach as evidence-based medicine. It helps organizations create consistency in their leadership. (Doesn't it seem funny that we happily standardize everything from the use of our logo to the brand of cafeteria trays we purchase, but we often struggle to standardize leadership practices?) EBL allows an organization to spread best practices throughout an organization, provide the best medical care possible, and have the greatest impact on the operational bottom line. It creates consistency, healthcare's most elusive outcome.

Of course, you're most likely doing many of these practices already. That's good. We find that the great majority of organizations feel alignment, communication, and accountability are the areas in which impact can be made. The good always want to be better. And that, of course, is what this book is all about.

Some time back I was asked to present at an organization. In order to better individualize the material, I created a survey to assess key critical factors in the organization. While the answers were not a total surprise to the leaders, the gap between some members of the organization's senior leadership team and between the different layers of leadership was greater than expected. The survey results have been vital to organizations taking action to achieve better performance.

This 16-question organizational assessment helps to diagnose exactly where the organization stands in regard to understanding the external environment and how leaders feel about certain key components critical to the success of any organization. We will examine these questions, one by one, as we proceed through the first part of this book:

What is your role?

Please list the top three things your organization does well and should continue to do.

Please list the top three opportunities for improvement at your organization.

What are the top three barriers/challenges you face that keep you from achieving your results in your area of responsibility at your organization?

Over the past five years, the external healthcare market in your area has been:
1=Very Easy
2=Easy
3=Normal
4=Difficult
5=Very Difficult

Over the next five years, the external healthcare market in your area will be:
1=Very Easy
2=Easy
3=Normal
4=Difficult
5=Very Difficult

If your organization continues as it is today (with same processes, cost structure, efficiencies, patient care volume, productivity, and techniques), the results over the next five years will be:
1=Much Worse
2=Worse
3=Same
4=Better
5=Much Better

How well does your current leadership training prepare you for your leadership role?
1=Very Poor
2=Poor
3=Fair
4=Good
5=Excellent

How many employees do you directly supervise (complete their annual evaluation)?

How many of those employees that you supervise are not meeting performance expectations?

How many employees do you have currently working for you who are in formal corrective/disciplinary action?

How well does your current leader evaluation system hold people accountable?
1=Very Poor
2=Poor
3=Fair
4=Good
5=Excellent

Rate your perception of the consistency in leadership throughout the organization.
(1=Worst to 10=Best in Class)

Rate the skill set at your organization in implementing and standardizing best practices throughout the organization.
(1=Worst to 10=Best in Class)

From a patient/family perspective and point of view, how would a patient/family rate your organization?
(1=Worst to 10=Best in Class)

Rate your perception of the ease of practicing medicine for physicians at your organization.
(1=Worst to 10=Best in Class)

For a downloadable copy of this organizational assessment and examples from other organizations, please visit www.studergroup.com/StraightALeadership.

When completing the assessment, we have the organization divide its leaders into categories and ask, "What is your role?" Most often we end up with three or four categories, depending on the organization's size and scope.

First, there is usually a team of "C-Suite" or senior leaders.

Another category consists of department directors, managers, and supervisors. Depending on the organization, the hierarchy may range from three to six layers deep. If the organization chooses, it also includes a physician group. Of course, an organization can include board of directors, staff, and volunteers. For this book, we will keep it simple.

Dividing leaders up this way allows us to evaluate how closely aligned the groups are in view of the external environment and the need to take action or change this behavior.

Job 1: Getting the True Picture

Here is a case study. We provided the assessment tool to 917 leaders as classified by the organization. The CEO sent the questions out and requested that everyone please complete them for use at an upcoming leadership session. As it turned out, *40 percent* of the leaders did not even commit and complete the assessments!

This is not an unusual response for an organization we've just started out with—but it is an indicator. The 60 percent response identifies an accountability issue.

Organizational Assessment

What is your role?

	# Responded	% Response Rate
Senior Leader	48	100%
Physician	30	18%
Department Director	153	79%
Manager	307	57%
Other	19	n/a
Total	**557** (917 = total)	**61%**

StuderGroup▼

Figure 1.1: Organizational Assessment - Role

If you're a C-Suite executive reading this you might say, "That would not happen to us." And you may be right. All your leaders *might* fill in the assessment. Then again, they might not. Why don't you take a shot at it? Without many reminders—just send it out once. Ask your leaders to complete the assessment and see how your organization does.

> We often see this lack of response by some leaders in the early stages of engagement as we assess alignment. We understand why it happens. Leaders have seen many programs come and go over the years. In fact, at times they have not completed an assignment and nothing has happened to them, so we've reinforced the reality that they don't need to do what we ask. We call this phenomenon: "What we permit, we promote."

For a downloadable copy of the Permit/Promote Exercise and more on this subject, visit www.studergroup.com/StraightALeadership.

This lack of response is understandable particularly when the leaders see the assessment questions come from an outside source. Their first reaction might be to say, "Oh my, another program, another initiative! Give me the t-shirt. Give me the pizza. Call me in a few years after this fails, too. When are they going to learn?"

Setting the Stage

When conducting an assessment to diagnose Alignment, Action, and Accountability, we start by seeking feedback from responders in three main areas. We want to know what they feel the organization does well, what opportunities for improvement they see, and what they view as the barriers to achieving higher performance.

These initial questions reveal a number of insights into the organization. For instance, does the role of a leader make a difference in how he or she categorizes an organization's strengths and weaknesses? Do objective data support the perceptions of the leaders? Are the barriers root causes of the organization's challenges or are they symptoms of them? Are there silos?

Our first question we ask after identifying their role, focuses on what leaders believe their organization is already doing well.

Organizational Assessment

Please list the top three things your organization does well and should continue to do.

Senior Leader	Physician	Department Director	Manager	Other
Quality of Care	Quality of Care	Quality of Care	Quality of Care	Quality of Care
Financial Performance (net revenue, EBITA, etc.)	Leadership	Patient Satisfaction/ Perception of Care	Patient Satisfaction/ Perception of Care	Patient Safety
Patient Satisfaction/ Perception of Care	Education Opportunities	Financial/ Fiscal Responsibility	Patient Safety	Patient Satisfaction/ Perception of Care

StuderGroup

Figure 1.2: Organizational Assessment – Top Things Organization Does Well

As illustrated by the results on the previous page, some common themes emerge. For example, no matter which organization completes this survey, most groups list patient care as a top three item. Considering the fact that providing patient care is the organization's reason for existing, the answer is not surprising. However, there is often a disconnect between leader perception of strong patient care and the reality revealed the objective data.

In our work we find that all organizations list quality patient care as a strength even if the mortality data, quality core measures, and patient's perception of care do not equate to excellence or high quality. We don't belabor this point, however, as the goal is to move to action.

Interestingly, senior teams are very good at listing financial stewardship as a strength when operating income is at goal or better, and not listing it as a strength if it is not. Yet they may list other areas as strengths even if the data is not at goal or even below average. As we'll discuss elsewhere in this book, finance departments are better at objective measurement as it relates to perception of performance than are other areas of healthcare.

Room for Improvement

Our next question asks leaders to list the top three opportunities for improvement at their organization.

Organizational Assessment

Please list the top three opportunities for improvement at your organization.

Senior Leader	Physician	Department Director	Manager	Other
Accountability	Communication	Dealing with Low Performance	Communication (transparent and open)	Dealing with Low Performance
Communication (transparent and open)	Process Improvements (i.e. billing, scheduling, etc.)	Accountability	Dealing with Low Performance	Communication (transparent and open)
Dealing with Low Performance	Customer and Patient Satisfaction	Communication (transparent and open)	System/Silo Thinking	Accountability

StuderGroup▼

Figure 1.3: Organizational Assessment – Top Opportunities for Improvement

This question also turns up common themes. Holding people accountable, dealing with performance issues, and communication seem to be on each organization's list. Our data shows that communication is mentioned by managers/supervisors 100 percent of the time, but not to that degree at the senior leader level.

It is noted also that "silo thinking" is identified as a problem by department leaders and managers/supervisors more often than by the senior leader group. This is not unusual as this group benefits when interdepartmental works run well and also sees the negative impact more closely when they do not.

The good news is this question very much helps the leadership team outline what actions need to be taken to close these perceptual (and often real) gaps that exist between senior leaders, department directors, and managers/supervisors.

Digging Deeper into the Challenges

Finally, we ask leaders to identify the main barriers and challenges that prevent them from achieving results.

Organizational Assessment

What are the top three barriers/challenges you face that keep you from achieving your results in your area of responsibility at your organization?

Senior Leader	Physician	Department Director	Manager	Other
Time and Priorities	Time and Priorities	Time and Priorities	Time and Priorities	Time and Priorities
Resources (financial, staff, space)	Resources (financial, staff, space)	Resources (financial, staff, space)	Resources (financial, staff, space)	Resources (financial, staff, space)
Economy and Financial Issues	Economy and Financial Issues	System/Silo Thinking	Communication	Communication

StuderGroup▼

Figure 1.4: Organizational Assessment – Top Barriers/Challenges

Answers to this question tend to show great consistency among leaders. Number one with department directors and managers/supervisors will be time, or more accurately, *not enough* time. At that point always have the group complete an exercise that reveals whether the real issue is "time" or "skill."

We often discover that what leaders are calling a "time" issue really boils down to a lack of skill, communication, teamwork, and accountability (which creates the need for more time spent than is ideal in most areas). So skill development that creates consistency in leadership will create more time. Skill is often the root cause of the issue; nonproductive time is the symptom.

When people complete the time exercise, they often find that they spend three to four times more time in unproductive hours than in productive hours.

Time Exercise

Where do you spend your time each week?

How many hours per week do you spend in unproductive meetings?	
How many hours per week do you spend handling interdepartmental issues?	
How many hours per week do you spend dealing with low performers?	
How many hours per week do you spend handling customer complaints?	
How many hours per week do you spend handling tool and equipment issues?	
Total hours in one week:	
How many hours per week do you spend in productive meetings?	
How many hours per week do you spend on reward and recognition of staff?	
How many hours per week do you spend on development of staff?	
Total hours in one week:	

StuderGroup▼

Figure 1.5: Time Exercise

For a downloadable copy of the Time Exercise, visit www.studergroup.com/StraightALeadership.

Only when other leadership skills are in place can an organization take full advantage of time management. You will read specifics on this later, but here is one example. Across the board, leaders say they go to too many meetings—specifically, too many less than fully productive meetings. When they are asked if the organization has a meeting template, standardized meeting management action, and mandatory leader training (as well as validation that all leaders can effectively lead meetings), the answer is *no*.

To access new meeting agendas and templates, visit www.studergroup.com/StraightALeadership.

So *is* it a "too many meetings" issue? Perhaps, but the bigger problem may be too many poorly led meetings that come from the fact that the organization doesn't have standardized meeting templates and leaders skilled in facilitating meetings.

Another item often identified is a lack of resources, with *staff* being mentioned again and again. Here, we always note that the most effective organizations outperform others. And in our experience, staffing and resources do not drive organizational performance, nor do a shortage of them detract from it. The best performing organizations are often the most efficient. The real contributing factors are lack of Alignment, reluctance to standardize best practices (Action), and unwillingness to validate high performance and address low performance (Accountability). Thus, the birth of this book.

It's particularly noteworthy if the senior leader team often includes time and resources on their lists. When this happens, the perception cascades throughout the organization and eventually creates a pervasive excuse mentality.

Asking these questions early on sets us up to ask later questions centering on evaluations, skill development or training, consistency, best practices, and performance management. Before we get into these specific issues, though, we focus on context—determining how leaders view the larger world in which their organization must operate.

Looking Outside: How Leaders See the External Environment

Here is the first question beyond the strengths, opportunities, and barriers questions in our organizational assessment that analyzes alignment. Leaders are asked to rate the external environment in their market area over the last five years. The rankings go from 1 to 5 with 1 being *very easy*, 2 *easy*, 3 *normal*, 4 *difficult*, and 5 *very difficult*.

Organizational Assessment

Over the past five years, the external healthcare market in your area has been:

		Very Easy 1	Easy 2	Normal 3	Difficult 4	Very Difficult 5
Senior Leader	68.2	0	1	15	28	4
Physician	67.5	0	0	14	11	5
Department Director	63.1	1	8	62	74	8
Manager	60.3	1	13	156	133	4
Other	61.8	0	1	10	6	2
Total	62.2	2	23	257	252	23

* Calculation: 1=0, 2=25, 3=50, 4=75, 5=100

StuderGroup▼

Figure 1.6: Organizational Assessment – External Environment Past Five Years

To calculate results, we assign each rating a numerical value: *1* equals 0, *2* equals 25, *3* equals 50, *4* equals 75, and *5* equals 100. Then, by adding up the total and dividing by the number of respondents, we can get an average score for each group of respondents. This allows us to compare and contrast the rankings given by, for instance, senior leaders and department directors.

Usually, with this looking back question there is a small disconnect or a slight gap between the senior leaders and the rest of the organization. This gap shows that, in the past, senior leaders may have not communicated enough of what is happening in the external environment to the managers and supervisors.

Many leaders withhold external information with the best of intentions. Senior leaders carry a lot of the weight in leadership, strategic planning, and dealing with the external environment, so the rest of the organization can make sure that everything is happening every single day to provide the best patient care. But this philosophy may lead an organization into less than the desired operating performance.

Often, leaders don't tell the rest of the workplace exactly what is going on because they don't want to burden them. *That's my job*, they think. But good intentions don't always mean good results.

People may not put full effort into the *how* if they don't know the *why*. "Do it because I said so," might be a favorite parental phrase, but we all know it's not a good leadership technique! Directives can seem arbitrary and even pointless to employees who are being kept in the dark about the *why*. Most supervisors and employees want that information very much so they can perform better.

Facts Are Friendly.

The lack of in-depth communication on the external environment can cause perception issues between some senior leaders who are pushing for internal changes to respond to outside pressures and other senior leaders, managers, and supervisors who don't see the urgency for the changes. These leaders begin to believe that they are being micromanaged.

> The results of this question explain why in the past changes may not have been implemented as quickly as the senior leaders want. It's not that managers and supervisors don't have the skill level to deal with the external environment—it's that they may not completely understand the seriousness of the situation. The senior leaders face the more the difficult challenge of getting everyone on the same page. And the first step is coming to the realization that yes, they *can* handle the facts.

Some years back I spoke at a multi-hospital organization. It was the first time that the entire organization had brought every leader together. Before then, we had worked with one small component of the organization. During the first break, some leaders came up to me to say they felt the chief financial officer was micromanaging everyone. Getting replacement staff and a piece of equipment had been made much tougher.

I met with the CFO and asked a number of operational questions. Some of my questions were basic, such as how they were doing financially. I asked about their debt capacity. The CFO mentioned that they were in the process of building one replacement facility. They were going to use all of their borrowing capabilities until that facility went online and started producing results.

I asked how many days of cash on hand they had, followed by how many days of cash on hand they needed to avoid being in default of their bonds. It turned out they were running extremely close. I asked him if he was concerned about that and he said absolutely. Then I asked, "Is everybody in the room in a leadership position aware of this?" His reply: "I don't think so."

See, in the past leaders may have kept that type of information in the C-Suite or the upper echelons of the organization—and again, maybe for good reason. *What will people do with the data?* leaders may have wondered. *Is it necessary for anyone to know? What will happen if the supervisors and employees know how tight things are? What if the media knows? The physicians? Our patients? Our competitors?*

These are valid questions. But the challenge is that if the solution-finders are not aware of the situation, the organization won't get the ideas, the sense of urgency, and the performance it needs. They *can* handle the facts.

When I got up to speak, I had the CFO come up on the stage. I interviewed him much the same way that I had already done privately. We talked about exactly what was going on and why he was managing the finances so tightly. When we were done, everybody realized, well *this* is why overtime is being limited. This is why we're not able to just hire replacements without justifying it. This is why capital equipment purchases are so tight.

Their perception was that the CFO was just being tight, when the reality was that he had a good reason. In fact, he was doing everything he could to help the organization be successful, so they could get staff, so they could get equipment, so they could reinvest in their future. However, without a clear explanation, the sides just were not aligned. This causes a disconnect within the leadership ranks—a disconnect that cascades throughout the organization.

What Does the Future Hold?

Next, leaders are asked to project ahead half a decade. Do they see the external environment being *very easy, easy, normal, difficult,* or *very difficult* over the next five years?

Organizational Assessment

Over the next five years, the external healthcare market in your area will be:

		Very Easy 1	Easy 2	Normal 3	Difficult 4	Very Difficult 5
Senior Leader	85.4	0	0	0	28	20
Physician	80.0	0	0	3	18	9
Department Director	80.2	1	3	12	84	53
Manager	73.4	2	5	63	178	59
Other	76.3	0	1	4	7	7
Total	76.8	3	9	82	315	148

* Calculation: 1=0, 2=25, 3=50, 4=75, 5=100

StuderGroup▾

Figure 1.7: Organizational Assessment – External Environment Next Five Years

Again, we calculate results by assigning values to the ratings: *1*=0, *2*=25, *3*=50, *4*=75, and *5*=100. So in the assessment results above, senior leaders' answers averaged out to a value of 85.4—between "Difficult" and "Very Difficult," in other words.

This is always interesting. We find that the C-Suite, the senior leaders, tend to view the external environment much in the same way, and usually they understand it very well. And why? Well, it's not unusual for a senior leader to get four or five online publication updates per day, from their associations, research centers, or magazines.

I read these updates myself, and the main theme is discouraging. Very rarely have I ever opened an email that said, "Good news! Medicare is paying more! Good news! Medicaid is paying more! Good news! Our self-pay individuals have all found financial wealth and will be paying all of their bills. Good news! The vendors will be calling to lower their costs because they know we are in turbulent times!"

Yes, what most of us read in the C-Suite boils down to the reality that things are getting tougher and tougher and tougher.

When I do sessions, I ask the C-Suite if they receive these daily doses of joy and they raise their hands. However, when I ask managers and supervisors, I get a different response. Very few hands go up.

Recently, I asked a nurse manager if she sees those updates. She said she doesn't. She is so busy figuring out how to staff three shifts, 365 days a year, 24 hours a day, how to deal with call-ins, and how to improve patient care that she really does not have time to see what is happening externally. She's just trying to figure out how to make it through *this* day.

A Matter of Perspective

When people are at different spots in the organization, they are naturally going to see things differently based upon their position. The goal here is to get everybody seeing external forces the same way.

After all, if you live right on the beach, you're going to see that hurricane hitting. If you live further inland and can't see the waves crashing down on the beach, you might think it's a nice day!

Like any good organization or any good association, whether it's a theatre troupe, an athletic team, or a wedding party, success depends on how aligned everyone is. If leaders don't get everyone to align, they won't get the performance they need. And research (not to mention common sense) tells us that if everyone doesn't have the same information, alignment is nearly impossible.

In the example illustrated by Figure 1.7, the senior leaders rated the external environment over the next five years as *difficult* or *very difficult*. Most physicians and department directors rated it as *difficult* or *normal*. Believe it or not, a few directors even rated it *easy* or *very easy*. Overall, the managers and supervisors rated the external environment more normal than their leaders did. Sure, some rated it *difficult* but not nearly the same percentage as senior leaders.

See the disconnect?

What If Nothing Changes? (The Expectations Gap and How It Throws Off Alignment)

The next question asks what results leaders expect over the next five years if the organization continues as it is today: the same staffing patterns, the same techniques, the same tools, generally the same philosophy. The rating scale is 1 *much worse,* 2 *worse,* 3 *same,* 4 *better,* and 5 *much better.* (As always, we calculate the scores by assigning numerical values to the ratings: *1*=0, *2*=25, *3*=50, *4*=75, and *5*=100.)

Organizational Assessment

If your organization continues as it is today (with the same processes, cost structure, efficiencies, patient care volume, productivity, and techniques), the results over the next five years will be:

		Much Worse 1	Worse 2	Same 3	Better 4	Much Better 5
Senior Leader	38.5	5	21	13	9	0
Physician	44.2	1	10	14	5	0
Department Director	43.0	7	59	57	30	0
Manager	46.1	7	107	125	63	5
Other	44.7	0	9	6	3	1
Total	44.4	20	206	215	110	6

* Calculation: 1=0, 2=25, 3=50, 4=75, 5=100

StuderGroup▼

Figure 1.8: Organizational Assessment – External Environment If Organization Continues As It Is Today

The answers are often a real eye-opener for the C-Suite. The findings shown in Figure 1.8, for example, show that 54 percent of senior leaders—presumably because they are the closest to the external environment—believe results will be *much worse* or *worse*. More physicians and department directors than senior leaders said results will be *the same* or *better*. More of the frontline supervisor managers, 63 percent, say they'll be *the same, better,* or *much better*.

This organization was about to make many changes due to a decrease in reimbursements and declining investment income. Yet over half of the leaders, including some of the senior leaders—331 out of 557 respondents—said that if the healthcare system continued to operate the same way, the results for the next five years would be *the same, better,* or *much better.*

An organization that's not aligned at the senior leadership level will certainly never be aligned on other levels. Let's say the CEO is deeply concerned about the external environment, but the CNO thinks everything is okay. Well, the CNO's perception may lead the people she reports to—which make up a large part of the organization—to assume the CEO is overreacting. They'll just keep doing things the same way.

As a result, the problems caused by the misalignment at the top will multiply as they cascade down through the hierarchy. They'll get worse, not better.

> Here's a good way to think about the importance of alignment. If a pilot changes the longitude and latitude of his coordinates even slightly, the plane will land in the wrong town. (When Christopher Columbus was trying to get to the Indies, he had the wrong longitude and latitude. He ended up in South America and didn't even realize it!)

This happens in organizations, too. Executives can underestimate the big impact even a small misalignment can have on an organization. They make the mistake of being satisfied with "sort of close" instead of insisting on "right on."

Standing Still on a "Down" Escalator

Healthcare today is like standing still on a downward moving escalator. If the organization stays the same, it will continue moving down and things will just get worse.

When I was president of a hospital, we announced a pay raise. Everybody got excited. We stated what the pay raise was and gave the number, which totaled close to $2 million. Of course, people were pleased. Then we said, "Okay, now we've got to figure out how to reduce expenses or increase our revenue in order to pay for this." Suddenly, it was a different story.

Many times there is a disconnect in people's minds between getting a pay raise and how the organization funds it. The money has to come from somewhere. The same is true when we buy a piece of equipment: We have to take the funds from something or increase revenues to pay for it.

So the ability to connect the dots is important. Leaders must help their organization understand they are in a continuous performance improvement process. Organizations must consistently be more successful than they have been in the past.

The numbers in Figure 1.8 reveal an organization in which the senior leader team sees things differently from everyone else. Sixty-three percent of the manager and supervisor group believe they can keep up the status quo and everything will be okay.

Sometimes, It Takes Pain to Make Us Pay Attention.

In 2004, I and many others learned firsthand about human nature and the external environment—specifically, our reluctance to adapt to outside changes.

I live on Pensacola Beach in Florida, and we were right in the path of Hurricane Ivan, a Category 3 storm. At its peak in the Gulf of Mexico, Ivan was the size of the state of Texas. It spawned 117 tornadoes across the eastern U.S. causing $13 billion worth of damage. Twenty-five people died, 14 of them in Florida.

Now, let's talk about the context: Hurricane Ivan churned in the Gulf of Mexico for two weeks. The Weather Channel broadcasted updates on the storm several times every hour. There was no shortage of information on the size and potential danger of this massive hurricane. People had plenty of warning that there was a high probability it would make landfall in or near our area.

However, it had been nine years since the last hurricane had hit the Pensacola area. Locals had forgotten the devastation. Thousands (myself included) had moved to our community since the last storm and had never experienced a hurricane. People were accustomed to near misses that veered to the east or west of Pensacola Beach.

Some people boarded up their homes and bought food, water, and hurricane supplies. Others made hotel reservations in Montgomery, Birmingham, and Atlanta and left as Hurricane Ivan approached Pensacola.

However, many did not evacuate and did not buy the necessary supplies to survive the weeks without electricity. They lived to regret their decisions. Due to the wrath of Ivan, homes that had survived hurricanes for more than four decades were completely destroyed.

Ten months later, Hurricane Dennis hit our area approximately 30 miles to the east of where Hurricane Ivan had made landfall. This time, most of the community evacuated. This time, they understood the very real danger. Hurricane Dennis was not as bad as Hurricane Ivan, but this time no one doubted the external environment.

What is the difference in these two situations? The news media handled both similarly. Residents knew each time that a dangerous hurricane was heading straight for them. However, when Hurricane Dennis approached Pensacola Beach, the entire community saw the external environment the same way. There was no disconnect between emergency management leaders and the general public.

Unfortunately, it took the painful experience of Hurricane Ivan to get everyone on the same page.

The same is true in healthcare. There are times when we react to a change in the external environment only after we've had painful experiences. Much of that pain is unnecessary, and pain that *is* necessary can be reduced. Although it's still painful to deal with changes in the external environment, we can alleviate the pain by executing actions quickly and properly.

Of course, quick and proper execution requires all leaders, across the organization, to be on the same page. Alignment is what keeps organizations from having to learn the hard way.

Yes, We've Overcome Obstacles in the Past. But Are We Victims of Our Own Success?

Senior leaders need to continually educate managers and supervisors and cascade that information throughout the organization, including the medical staff. Many senior leaders may believe this has already been done because they downloaded tons of information. Of course, downloading is not enough.

Recently I saw a healthcare organization newsletter in which the CEO outlined all of the negative things that were going on externally in our industry at the national level. It was impressive. Unfortunately there was no connection to what the information meant to readers. The article didn't mention the impact these external changes would have specifically to that organization and what readers could do to control their own damage.

Our research finds leaders and staff often fail to grasp the severity of this "disconnect" problem. There is a reason for disbelief. Leaders have told their employees that the sky is falling before and no one wants to believe the message or the extent of the change needed. Plus, senior leaders have shown great ability to navigate tough waters in the past.

> Over the last four decades, the healthcare industry has gone through many things that we thought would negatively impact organizations. Many of them have. However, we've also learned through creativity, innovation, intelligence, strongly committed employees and physicians, and excellent leadership that healthcare organizations could adjust to many of these changes.

Leaders first heard these warnings years ago when Medicare came in. Later, physicians began moving certain procedures into their office settings, which threatened the acute care environment. When ambulatory care started one-day surgeries, panic set in. Horror stories of patients leaving with IV drips began to make the rounds.

Hospitals, of course, adjusted and today one-day surgery patients are the most satisfied in the healthcare setting. Why? We changed how we operate. Organizations implemented pre-visit communications to better explain procedures, because care providers don't have a lot of time with patients. They also do post-surgery follow-up calls to make sure medications are understood as well as home care instructions.

Then came the rise of systems. Hospital leaders looked at ways to combine purchasing, information technology, and managed care negotiations. This led to the formation of several large healthcare systems. Many hospitals did not necessarily want to be part of a larger system, but they also saw the advantages.

And lo and behold, research today tells us that most larger systems operate more efficiently than stand-alones. However, even though the decision was sound, it creates anxiety in hospitals. Success still must come down to execution. And certain stand-alone, independent hospitals have figured out a way to weather the storm and be successful.

But whether you are part of a small stand-alone hospital, an integrated system of smaller hospitals, a large regional network, or a national vertically integrated chain, it all comes down to how well your organization executes.

So we've gone through re-engineering, managed care, capitation, nursing shortages, and the Balanced Budget act. Remember back in the 1990s being convinced that the Balanced Budget act would cause such tremendous damage that the industry would never survive? Of course it did, and today yields better clinical outcomes than ever before.

All of this illustrates how good healthcare leadership has been. It's clear that many healthcare providers have learned to adjust and do well in dealing with all these external changes. However—and this is a big however—many healthcare organizations may be victims of their successful adaptability.

As Jim Collins says in his book *Good to Great*, some of the prediction of failure is past success. Because organizations have gone through these challenges and done pretty well in adapting to the external environment, managers and staff might think, "Here we go again. Things are not as bad as senior leaders say. We'll get through this just like we have in the past."

But is this necessarily true? Will leaders always be able to pull an organization's collective behind out of the fire? The belief that "someone up there" will always be able to figure it out—a belief that can breed a risky complacency—is what I've heard called "Park Ranger Leadership."

Park Ranger Leadership Creates Dependency.

I was first introduced to Park Ranger Leadership by consultant Bob Wilson when I was at Holy Cross Hospital in Chicago. We were frustrated with managers not moving quickly enough and had a desire to improve communication.

He basically said, "I have good news and bad news for you. The good news is you have a strong senior leadership team that is helping you do pretty well in a very difficult environment.

"The bad news is you are not setting up the managers for continued success because you've created a co-dependent relationship. Your senior leadership is so strong that the managers sit back and wait for someone to tell them what to do. In essence, without even realizing it, you have taken some creativity away from the organization. Your strength is also your weakness."

This concept has been coined "Park Ranger Leadership."

I think a personal story illustrates the point.

I went camping with three of my grandsons, Cooper, Caiden, and Quin, ages eight to four. I was pretty nervous taking the three boys, especially after getting the directions from their mothers, my daughter and my daughter-in-law. I found out quickly that an overnight camping trip is a pretty complex situation.

After making it through the first night in the Wisconsin Dells, we went hiking that next day. The boys were excited to see a deer as we walked and we were having a lot of fun.

After awhile, though, I got a little disoriented and wasn't sure how to get back to the campsite. My grandsons were getting a little tired and wanted to go back. I was trying to keep them occupied without letting them know I was sort of lost.

Eventually, we found the way out of the forest, a different way from how we got in. We ended up on a highway and followed it back to the campgrounds.

The experience helped me understand the Park Ranger Leadership phenomenon in a very literal way.

You see, when we were lost, I had to figure out how to get back to the campground. My grandsons depended on me. But let's get hypothetical for a moment. What if a park ranger had come along and told me he had spotted us? What if he told us park rangers were stationed throughout the park? What if he then led us out of the woods?

Well, I would still have been tired and anxious, but I would have been very grateful. And on some level, I would have started depending on that park ranger. To me it might have seemed that the park ranger's job was to lead me out of the forest.

Let's say some time goes by and I'm back camping again in another campground—this time without my grandsons. I go for a hike and get a little disoriented and lost again (I can hear you thinking, *Gosh, he gets lost a lot!*). Yes, I am anxious, but in the back of my mind I'm also thinking that the last time this happened, a park ranger showed up. Sure enough, after about half an hour, here he comes. I'm grateful as the park ranger shows me the way back to the campground.

Now (to continue on our hypothetical journey), some time goes by and I return to the woods. Of course, not being the smartest guy in the world, I get disoriented and soon am lost *again*. What do I do this time? I've talked to thousands of people in healthcare, and when I share this analogy, they normally say, "If it were me and a park ranger had rescued me twice, I would probably sit down and at least wait a half hour to see if the park ranger came before I started trying to find my own way out. I may even be upset if the ranger did not show up right away."

> Many leaders in healthcare have, with all good intentions, created a park ranger mentality in their organizations. Every day as I travel the country, I am impressed by the strong leadership in healthcare. However, that very strength

almost takes away the need for other people in the organization to urgently seek solutions to problems created by a changing external environment.

So ask yourself, *Have I created some Park Ranger Leadership in my organization?* When people come up to you with a problem, perhaps it's time to start asking them, *What do you think we should do? What's your suggestion? If you were in my shoes, what decisions would you make? Everyone* needs to be a park ranger.

Interestingly, I've found that when you give the problem back to the person who's looking to you for a solution, he often finds the answer. The first time you ask him what he thinks you should do, he'll probably say, "I don't know." But persist. I learned from communication experts Peter Glaser, PhD, and Susan Glaser, PhD, to say, "But if you *did* know, *then* what would you do?" There's a good chance that he'll come right out with the answer.

I'm not sure how or why it works. The question must kick down some sort of psychological wall. But I've seen it in action enough times to know that most organizations are filled with brilliant problem solvers. It's up to leaders to help them find and empower their inner park ranger.

It's Time to Answer the Wake-up Call.

Today healthcare faces a tough environment, like we have faced in the past and surely will face again in the future. Leaders absolutely need to get as many people as possible on the same page they're on. The first section of the organizational assessment I've shared can be a tremendous wake-up call, proving beyond a doubt that senior leaders and the rest of their organization can have very different perceptions of the same problems. It can also reveal the need to better identify what the real problems are facing the organization and how deep they go.

If not dealt with properly, the task of making adjustments in the internal environment becomes like "cracking a whip" for the senior leaders and becomes a little too difficult for the directors, managers, and supervisors to execute.

It is a little too easy to just download information instead of helping people understand the data they have been given. In the hospital newsletter mentioned earlier, the CEO did an excellent job detailing the challenges healthcare faces in great detail, but he missed telling employees what they as individuals or the organization as a whole could do to meet them. Those employees will a) ignore the message, or b) (and this is worse) see themselves as victims since they don't know how to deal with problems brought on by the external environment.

It is imperative that senior leaders let managers and employees know through many discussions what is going on and how it impacts the organization—and what needs to be done in response.

SUMMARY

So far, we have covered the importance of alignment in dealing with changes in the external environment. Healthcare systems are aligned in regard to providing excellent medical care. However, in our work at Studer Group we have never, ever found any organization that's truly aligned in regard to dealing with these turbulent times—though certainly some are closer than others.

The first three questions we ask in our organizational assessment are: *Please list the top three things your organization does well and should continue to do; Please list the top three opportunities for improvement at your organization;* and *What are the top three barriers/challenges you face that keep you from achieving your results in your area of responsibility at your organization?*

The answers to these questions reveal that leaders typically have certain perceptions about their organization's strengths that are not supported by objective data. Also, it becomes obvious that leaders are more likely to notice the challenges that directly affect them. Finally, we often discover that what leaders perceive as a lack of time may actually be a lack of skill.

The next three questions we ask give the organization a very good idea of the gap between the senior leaders and the rest of the management team in terms of perceptions about the external environment and the sense of urgency in dealing with it.

Two of the questions center on leader perception of the difficulty of the external environment during the *past* five years and over the *next* five. Then, the next one asks what kind of results leaders predict for the organization over the next five years if it continues as it is today.

Sometimes as many as 50 percent of managers surveyed actually think if they continue to do what they're doing, the future is going to be the same, better, or even

much better. Perhaps they feel that way because in the past they've always adjusted successfully to changes. Or maybe they are feeling that way because the senior leadership team has great confidence in its own abilities to solve whatever problems may come.

Failure to align an organization in its responses to changes in the external environment can create an ineffective "Because I said so!" mentality. Senior leaders will become frustrated that managers and employees aren't implementing changes with the sense of urgency that they themselves feel. Managers and employees will become frustrated and resent what they perceive as being micromanaged.

As Jim Collins wrote, we can be victims of our own past successes. Healthcare leaders have had remarkable success in handling past upheavals in the external environment. There is a strong tendency to be complacent and believe we will weather these turbulent times without much effort.

Also, senior leaders need to be careful not to create a park ranger mentality among the managers. It's important to develop creativity among managers and get them involved in developing the solutions. Senior leaders can't continually come to their rescue.

Later in this book, I will share a number of tools that Studer Group has developed to help organizations successfully close that gap and keep the organization as aligned as possible. The bigger the gap between the C-Suite and the staff, the harder it will be for the organization to move in a unified pattern and ultimately achieve the desired performance.

CHAPTER TWO:

ACTION

*A*ction is the second "A" of leadership. How quickly and effectively leaders can drive action determines whether an organization lives or dies.

We've already discussed the speed at which the external environment changes these days. One might assume this means leaders have to take action immediately following the changes. Actually, the reality is even more daunting than that. Today's leaders must be able to anticipate the outcome of changes *even as they are occurring* and respond to them. No one can afford to be late to market. Only early adapters will thrive.

Of course leaders need great agility in order to see changes coming and adapt accordingly. And they must also have the right skill set. What this skill set might be depends on the organization's circumstances, but leaders must be able to keep the organization healthy and performing well.

Without action, it is impossible for an organization to improve. Sure, everyone might be aligned and have an understanding of their external environment—but if they don't have the right skill set with the needed urgency, the needed improvement will not happen or gains made will not be sustained.

Unfortunately, this is a common problem. Why? Because too many healthcare organizations have not spent enough time preparing their leaders for job success.

Let me give you a few statistics:

- The average healthcare leader gets 6.5 hours of pure leadership training per year.
- Of the Fortune 500 companies of the Top 100 Places to Work, none of them had less than 55 hours of leadership training.
- The great majority of the managers and supervisors in any organization—in fact, over 95 percent of them—do not have a master's degree in health administration or a master's degree in business administration. It's about on-the-job learning.

And it's not just published statistics that tell us leaders aren't getting the training they need. Leaders themselves typically admit that this is the case.

Many Leaders Feel Unprepared for the Job.

Remember the organizational assessment survey we started discussing in Chapter 1? The next question is, *How well does your current leadership training prepare you for your leadership role?* (In scoring it, a 5 is *excellent*, a 4 is *good*, a 3 is *fair*, a 2 is *poor*, and a 1 is *very poor*.) It's an important question to ask the leaders at your organization and one that is too often overlooked.

Organizational Assessment

How well does your current leadership training prepare you for your leadership role?

		Very Poor 1	Poor 2	Fair 3	Good 4	Excellent 5
Senior Leader	55.7	1	6	24	15	2
Physician	52.5	0	4	19	7	0
Department Director	56.2	6	23	59	57	8
Manager	55.2	13	42	134	104	14
Other	59.2	0	2	10	5	2
Total	55.5	20	77	246	188	26

* *Calculation: 1=0, 2=25, 3=50, 4=75, 5=100*

StuderGroup.▼

Figure 2.1: Organizational Assessment – Leadership Training

Remember, we calculate these types of assessments by assigning each rating a numerical value; *1* equals 0, *2* equals 25, *3* equals 50, *4* equals 75, and *5* equals 100. The graphic above shows that, in this case, all categories of respondents gave answers that averaged out to somewhere in the 50s—right around *fair* in other words.

Notice also that out of the 500-some people surveyed, only 26 felt that they were provided with excellent training. And clearly, even the people at the senior level—the ones who must approve the training—also recognize that it's not that great.

Leaders simply cannot be expected to perform better and implement different tools and techniques if they've never been trained to do so.

There is not a medical staff organization or medical association in the U.S. that has found a way to decrease the amount of time it takes to be re-certified in their specialty even though external environments have changed. Yet inside healthcare organizations, manager and staff training and development is usually one of the first things to go.

Take Ownership of Your Leadership Training.

And here's another disconnect. Often, senior executives delegate the important task of training to another department or individual. Delegating the training itself makes sense, of course, but delegating what the outcomes need to be does not. It's critical that senior leaders are on the same page with those who do the training regarding what skills their leaders need to have in order to achieve the desired results.

Over the years, Studer Group has developed what we call a Senior Leader Toolkit, which examines and diagnoses an organization's mentoring system. Its ultimate goal is for senior leaders to take ownership of training the group below them. That group must then take ownership of training the group below *them*—and so on. In other words, leader development should cascade through the organization.

Anyway, the Toolkit includes an exercise in which leaders judge their own skill set and others' leadership. Leaders are divided up into categories/roles. For this example, let's use three categories: Senior Leaders, Department Directors, and Frontline Supervisors.

Senior leaders usually include anyone who goes to some of the executive team meetings. They're usually folks with titles like VP, CEO, COO, CIO, CFO, CNO, CMO, CQO (Quality), and CHR (Human Resources). Business Development, Marketing, and Managed Care are some additional areas included at the senior leader table.

Department directors report to one of the C-Suite leaders. They may have a secretary or an administrative assistant, but most of their direct reports are people who supervise other people, the managers/supervisors. Of course, each organization can vary.

Frontline supervisors include managers, supervisors, and unit leaders. These individuals supervise hourly employees so they usually have a wider span of control and often more people to directly supervise.

On a flipchart, a recorder writes out each area. This is an exercise you might want to try, too.

The senior executives evaluate their skill set on a scale of 1 through 5 to the question, "How skilled is your team?"

I've been teaching this exercise since about 1997 and perhaps not surprisingly, I've never had an organization's senior executive team rank themselves lower than a 4.4. While some jokingly flash the high 5 to the group, the high score they do eventually give themselves makes sense to them. After all they are the highest paid individuals, highly educated, experienced, and at the senior leader table. That means they *should* have the most developed skill set, their thought process goes, which is why they rank themselves in the middle 4s.

Then senior leaders rank the skills of the level directly below them—the department directors. They tend to rank these employees in the 3s. Usually it's no lower than a 3.5 and no higher than a 3.8.

Next, the senior leaders assess their frontline supervisors and generally rank them in the 2s. It's at this point in the exercise that the discussion starts to get lively. A light bulb goes on for one of the executives, and he says, "Now I see it. We need supervisor training. Our frontline supervisors are the ones who really need the training and development." And if the HR person is there, they point and say, "We really need a supervisory training program in our organization."

Here are the results:

How do you rate skill sets of:	
Role	**Rating of Skill**
Senior Leader	4.5 - 5
Department Director	3 – 3.8
Frontline Supervisor	2 – 2.5

Now, take a moment and really look at this chart. Get yourself emotionally unengaged if you're thinking of your own team and ask yourself, *Is it possible to have a 4.5-rated senior leadership team and a 2.5-rated frontline supervisor team?*

That is like saying a teacher is really great even though the students are not doing well.

The reality is the goal of the senior executive team should be to make sure they have excellent frontline supervisors. So until they can get those frontline supervisors to a 4.5, *they themselves* can't be a 4.5.

Sure, a senior leader may deserve a high score in her own performance in certain areas. But in evaluating themselves, senior leaders can't exclude how well they mentor and develop the people who report to them. It's an integral part of the job—or at least it *should* be.

Now that does not mean you should not go ahead with the frontline supervisor training. You can and should. Just don't underestimate the power that you, their leader, can have. Round on your direct reports, hold regular supervisory meetings, and coach them. Sure, frontline supervisors can learn when they go to a classroom, and listen to someone talk about what a great leader looks like. But there is real magic when they see those qualities personified by the person they report to and/or the person who mentors them.

Performance Issues Keep Leaders Bogged Down.

Most leaders truly enjoy mentoring and developing the people who report to them. Very few of us enjoy the flipside: dealing with staff performance problems. In fact, the entire healthcare industry really struggles with this issue. I think it's because we are "healers" at heart—we simply don't want to give up on *anyone*, and that includes our low performers. (We'll talk more about this a little later.)

Obviously, though, if you want your organization to perform, you can't have performance issues bogging you down. Action must be taken. The first order of business is determining how serious a problem you have right now.

When we help organizations assess the extent of their performance issues, we ask three questions. The first one seems pretty straightforward at first glance: *How many employees do you directly supervise?*

Organizational Assessment

How many employees do you directly supervise (complete their annual evaluation)?

	#
Senior Leader	9.79
Physician	19.16
Department Director	25.9
Manager	28.44
Other	6.63
Total (includes all raw data)	**20.91**

StuderGroup▼

Figure 2.2: Organizational Assessment – Number of employees supervised

Actually, this question typically requires some explanation. Some leaders think they supervise 100, 500, or even 1,000 employees because they look at the question in the context of their whole cascade approach. We help them simplify that number by explaining to them that the word "supervise" means *direct supervision*, and that direct supervision entails doing an employee's schedule and/or performing her annual evaluation.

We find senior executives supervise fewer people than frontline supervisors. On average when we add them all up we find that in a non-academic healthcare system the average leader supervises 20.8 people, particularly if he is not a working supervisor.

We also work with medical groups, hospices, various home care agencies, and long-term care facilities where the number might be even more than that. Still, our research shows that no matter what organization we go to, the average lands somewhere between 20 and 21.

Of course, determining the exact number is not our main goal. We just use it to set the stage for the next two questions.

The next question we ask on our organizational assessment focuses on the number of employees who aren't meeting performance expectations.

Organizational Assessment

How many of those employees whom you supervise are not meeting performance expectations?

	#
Senior Leader	0.46
Physician	1.23
Department Director	2.5
Manager	3.5
Other	0.47
Total	**1.85**

(557 x 1.85 = 1030.45)

StuderGroup©2009

Figure 2.3: Organizational Assessment – Performance Expectation (557 leaders)

The average answer to this organizational assessment question is about 1.8. In other words, the typical leader has at least one person working for him who is not meeting performance expectations. Some may have none; some may have more.

When I do an on-site speaking engagement, I like to ask groups, "How many of you have ever inherited someone you would never rehire because of a performance issue?" It never fails that pretty much everybody raises his or her hand.

Then, I ask them if they've ever noticed that when they hear complaints about those individuals, they are quick to point out that they did not hire that person.

Of course, the reality is that if a supervisor keeps a low performing employee for one year and gives him a good evaluation, she *has* in effect "rehired" that low performer.

Now, you might be thinking that having one or two low performers is not that big of a deal. But do a bit of math and you'll see a disheartening picture emerge. As Figure 2.3 shows, at one organization 557 leaders responded. Since each one supervises approximately 1.85 low performers, this particular organization has more than a thousand employees who are not meeting expectations!

What We Permit, We Promote. (And We're "Promoting" Low Performance!)

Next we ask our participants how many employees they have working for them who are currently undergoing corrective or disciplinary action.

Organizational Assessment

How many employees do you have currently working for you who are in formal corrective/disciplinary action?

	#
Senior Leader	0.13
Physician	0.13
Department Director	1.1
Manager	1.42
Other	0.05
Total	**0.66**

(557 x .66 = 367.62)

StuderGroup

Figure 2.4: Organizational Assessment – Disciplinary Action (557 leaders)

Studer Group has performed this survey with many organizations. And we've found that between 40 to 60 percent of employees identified by their manager as "not meeting expectations" are not in any performance counseling. There is no documentation in their personnel file. They are not engaged in any due disciplinary process.

In short, most healthcare leaders agree they need to do better in dealing with their low performance issues. The reasons I hear for not taking action are, "Human Resources won't let me," or, "The union protects them." Both are not found to be true. We have found that in both cases, the real issue is lack of documentation.

> "What we permit, we promote." Leaders have essentially told **60** percent of their low performing employees that their behavior is okay. They've said, "We're not going to write you up. We're not going to address these issues. And in fact, at the end of the year, we'll just give you a good evaluation."

This is, of course, a serious problem. This entire book is focused on responding to the hurricane of outside forces battering our industry. But no organization can respond to its *external* environment without addressing the *internal* one. Ultimately, success depends on how well an organization can execute—and that means addressing the employee performance issues that will sabotage excellence.

For a downloadable copy of the Permit/Promote exercise, please visit www.studergroup.com/StraightA-Leadership.

Why We Struggle with "Tough Love"

As we've been discussing, healthcare professionals struggle with low performers. Our industry is loaded with passionate—and *compassionate*—people. At times our DNA almost prevents us from dealing with performance issues. What makes us good at the work of healing holds us back from weeding out problem employees.

> Healthcare people are trained to never give up on anyone. We're trained to alleviate pain and take care of people. However, there are certain employees that we truly need to give up on. We need to stop taking care of them. We need to quit relieving their pain. It's the opposite of what we've been born to do. It's only by putting patient care and organizational performance above our own comfort that a leader can effectively deal with performance issues.

A physician once told me about the time a mortally injured child was brought into his ED. He went to work performing CPR and continued long after it was clear the child wouldn't be brought back to life. Eventually, his coworkers had to literally pull him away. He just did not want to give up. That's just how it is in all areas of healthcare. And that's why healthcare workers think that they can always do *something* to make someone successful.

Healthcare is filled with tremendous caregivers, and it's not just patients they care for. When you look at employee attitude surveys, you'll see that no matter how a person feels about the rest of the organization, the number one factor she consistently values is her relationships with her fellow coworkers. In fact, in a work environment that can at times be very emotionally draining, coworker relationships are often the most enjoyable part of the job.

A lady told me one time, almost crying, that she spent more time with her coworkers than she did with her family. She wasn't saying it in a negative way, mind you. She was grateful for her coworkers because they made her life and her profession so enjoyable. Healthcare people are relationship people who don't give up. That's why we as leaders must remind them—and ourselves—that dealing effectively with low performers allows the rest of the staff to create the best possible work environment and provide the best possible patient care.

Using Pain to Motivate Change

Healthcare leaders are also trained to alleviate pain. Ninety-two percent of healthcare employees greatly appreciate the fact that their leaders alleviate their pain with training, coaching, and mentoring, and they consistently respond well to these efforts. However, the other 8 percent—the staff members with serious performance problems—actually need to feel quite a bit of pain before they will change their behavior. We wish it wasn't this way, but it is.

Leaders who see performance problems within their organization often try everything to work them out. They try reward and recognition programs, employee transfers, new bosses, new schedules, new jobs—but for some people, the reality is leaders must allow them to feel the pain and consequences of their behavior.

> Employees with performance problems must realize that the pain of changing is less intense than the pain of staying the same.

The bottom line? Organizations need to help leaders overcome their natural tendency to alleviate pain by providing them with the tools and tactics they need to deal successfully with low performers.

But first, we need to make sure they're getting trained in the first place.

A Generation of Interim Leaders

As if all of these assessment findings aren't enough, healthcare leaders face one more challenge: Many of them were thrust into their current positions with virtually no training at all. In fact, they start out with a precursor for a job title—"Interim."

It's a common situation: A leader quits and the organization needs to move quickly to fill the position. So they appoint someone as the "interim" leader. Over time that person becomes the permanent leader, only she's never received the training she needs to do the job as effectively as possible.

When I travel the country and ask groups of healthcare leaders how they became leaders, many of them say, "My boss quit," or, "They just asked me one day." Many of them did not want the leadership position because— let's face it—being a leader in healthcare is pretty hard. But of course, once they accepted the job, they did the best they could under the circumstances.

Every employee within an organization is valuable. But the difference between being an hourly employee and being a leader is that the former has more control over his or her environment than the latter. Hourly employees know their schedule weeks in advance. They are more comfortable saying no to requests. If they have a family vacation planned and are asked to come in and work, they can decline. If they come in early or stay late, they're going to get paid a little bit extra. They know their hours, they know their pay, and they can plan their life around those factors.

This is not always the case for salaried employees. When they become leaders, their career move often translates to additional hours and sometimes less pay per hour. For some it may even mean having to pay more in out-of-pocket expenses for daycare and babysitters. Why would anyone want to trade in their freedom for more stress, longer hours, and possibly less pay per hour? They wouldn't, of course—which is why the healthcare industry had to get creative.

Of course, I am being a bit tongue-in-cheek here. Most people agree to become leaders because they want to make a big impact on the lives of others. Still, they rarely get the training they need to lead successfully. When I'm talking to groups about how long they've been the "interim" leader, they say, "Forever." And when I ask, "How much training did you get?" they say, "None," or, "Very little." (After all, why bother sinking a lot of money into an "interim" leader?)

Interim Leaders Can Too Often Maintain the Status Quo.

What do you think happens when a person becomes an "interim" leader? (Besides the lack of training, I mean?) The answer is complex.

If you think you're going to be in a leadership position for only a short period of time, why upset the applecart? If, say, there's a problem employee who needs to be dealt with, why would *you* deal with her? After all, in three to six months, you're just going to be her coworker again. So you just let it go.

When the interim position becomes permanent, the problem you've let go for so long now seems normal. And once that has happened, it's very hard to go back and make the necessary change.

I have a story from my own career that I believe illustrates how easy it is to get accustomed to the status quo. When I started working at Holy Cross, the organization had been and was struggling financially. And I noticed there was a lot of artwork on the wall, and each painting had a "For Sale" sign under it.

Now I understand why this happens. The paintings brighten up hospital décor, but they can be expensive. So the organization lets a company display paintings on its walls. When a piece of art sells, the hospital gets a percentage of the profits. It makes perfect sense to me and probably to you—but it may not make sense to patients and their families.

Imagine if you were a patient waiting for a procedure and you noticed "For Sale" signs under all the paintings. Wouldn't you think, *Wow, this hospital must be desperate if they're having to sell art to pay their bills! And they're getting ready to perform heart surgery on me? Yikes!*

See what I mean? When I arrived at Holy Cross I thought the For Sale signs on all the paintings and pictures sent the wrong message. So I decided to have the artwork removed. Unfortunately, Purchasing told me the hospital had a contract with the dealer who supplied the paintings and there was almost another year to go. In other words, we would just have to live with the artwork until then.

Anyway, for the next few months, everywhere I turned I saw a painting with a For Sale sign. It really bothered me. But as time passed, I started getting accustomed to the paintings. I even started getting fond of a few of them. For instance, in the snack shop there was one photo that contained all the World Series tickets from the beginning of baseball. I really enjoyed looking at this one.

One day, about eight months after I started at Holy Cross, I noticed the World Series piece was gone. I asked what happened and the snack shop manager informed me that someone had purchased it. I was actually a little upset. In fact, I was kicking myself for not having bought it myself when I had the chance!

Then, one Monday months later, I came into work and everything looked different. Had we painted? Finally I asked and was told that all the artwork was gone. The contract had finally run out—and I found myself missing the artwork!

I tell this story not to prove any particular point about artwork for sale in hospitals, but to illustrate a truth about human nature. We get so comfortable with the status quo that what at first seems unacceptable gradually starts to seem normal. It may not come to actually seem desirable, as the artwork did for me, but it may seem okay or at least familiar.

That's what happens to leaders. When they feel they don't have permission to make a change—or have the skill or the will to do so—they simply don't do it. As I said before, it's understandable. It's painful to instigate change when you're told you're going to be in your position for only a short period of time. But by not doing so, you set yourself up for failure.

Why? Because eventually someone will point out the big glaring problem you've let slide and they'll say, "You've been here for nine months. Why didn't you do something sooner?" No one will remember that you didn't have "permission" to make the change. They'll just notice that you didn't do it. And you probably won't get the long-term leadership position.

> My message to interim leaders is this: From day one, act like it's your real, permanent job. Don't wait to be given permission. Don't be a placeholder! Be a difference maker.

To senior leaders I would say: Be careful with interim titles. Empower your leaders. And *train* your leaders. If you don't, you are putting them at a real disadvantage. And of course the entire organization will ultimately pay the price.

SUMMARY

Action is the second "A" of leadership. Today's leaders must be able to anticipate the outcome of changes in the external environment *even as they are occurring* and respond with appropriate action. Only early adapters will survive.

Taking quick and effective action requires exceptional leadership. Unfortunately, many leaders don't have the skill sets they need.

One question Studer Group includes in its organizational assessment is, *How well does your current leadership training prepare you for your leadership role?* Generally, we find that very few leaders feel they receive sufficient training.

Ideally, leadership training cascades through an organization, with each leader taking ownership of training the leaders below him or her. However, this rarely happens in reality.

When Studer Group has a senior executive team evaluate its own skill set, most teams rate themselves somewhere between 4.5 and 5 (out of a possible 5). However, when we ask them to rate the leaders below them, they assign much lower numbers: 3.5-3.8 for department directors and 2-2.5 for frontline supervisors.

How can this be? Clearly senior leaders are not doing a great job of mentoring and developing the people below them.

One of the biggest problems leaders face? Low performers. Our organizational assessment has three questions that deal with this subject. They are: *How many employees do you directly supervise (complete their annual evaluation)? How many of the employees you supervise are not meeting performance expectations?* And *How many employees do you have currently working for you who are in formal corrective/disciplinary action?*

We typically find that the average leader has one or two employees who are not meeting performance expectations. However, of the employees identified as not meeting expectations, about 60 percent are not involved in any performance counseling. In other words, leaders aren't happy with these employees, but they're also doing nothing to improve their performance!

The same qualities that make healthcare professionals such wonderful caregivers also make them reluctant to "give up" on problem employees. Only good, solid leadership training can help them overcome this natural tendency to keep giving second chances.

And here's one more challenge: Healthcare organizations tend to appoint "interim leaders" and provide them with virtually no leadership training. Not surprisingly, interim leaders feel little ownership for their jobs. They tend to maintain the status quo—bad news for organizations trying to drive change.

CHAPTER THREE:

ACCOUNTABILITY

A *ccountability* is the third "A" of leadership. It's not hard to see why. An organization may be perfectly aligned in terms of how it plans to respond to the external environment. Its leaders may have the right skill sets that translate to the right actions. But if that organization doesn't have the systems in place to hold people accountable for those actions, none of this matters. Accountability is the glue that holds the best-laid plans together.

Part of the Leadership Diagnosis includes a series of questions designed to help the organization assess its own level of accountability.

What we find is that most organizations fully grasp the importance of accountability, and they put guidelines into place to hold people accountable *to*—but somehow, they fall short of closing the loop.

We ask the following question: *How well does your current leader evaluation system hold people accountable?* An answer of 5 is *excellent*, 4 is *good*, 3 is *fair*, 2 is *poor*, and 1 is *very poor*.

We average the responses in each category of leaders by assigning each rating a numerical value: *1* = 0, *2* = 25, *3* = 50, *4* = 75 and *5* = 100.

Organizational Assessment

How well does your current leader evaluation system hold people accountable?

		Very Poor 1	Poor 2	Fair 3	Good 4	Excellent 5
Senior Leader	43.8	3	17	18	9	1
Physician	50.0	1	4	20	4	1
Department Director	50.0	6	39	61	43	4
Manager	50.6	16	60	142	79	10
Other	50.0	1	4	9	4	1
Total	49.8	27	124	250	139	17

* Calculation: 1=0, 2=25, 3=50, 4=75, 5=100

StuderGroup▼

Figure 3.1: Organizational Assessment – Leader Evaluation

As you can see in Figure 3.1, the majority of respondents at this organization answered this question with a lukewarm *fair*. A fair performance evaluation creates fair outcomes; however, a fair performance is not what people expect in healthcare.

Another way to diagnose the effectiveness of your leader evaluation tool is to ask these questions: *Is it possible for a leader in your organization to not perform well but still get a good evaluation? In fact, is it possible for a leader in your organization to not meet his or her goals yet get an* excellent *evaluation?* If the answer to either of these questions is "yes," your organization will most likely not be able to achieve sustained high performance until you change how leaders are evaluated.

Competency Does Not Guarantee Good Execution.

Most organizations are working with inadequate evaluation systems. The healthcare industry has somehow fallen into the trap of using competency-based evaluation tools. And here's the problem: While these kinds of tools (obviously) measure competency, they simply don't hold leaders accountable for outcomes.

Competency isn't synonymous with good execution. Of course leaders need to be competent, but execution takes the ability to connect their skills to particular outcomes.

Poor evaluation tools in healthcare go hand in hand with poor execution. Why? Because poor evaluation tools keep leaders from seeing where improvements need to be made in their performance. Why should I change my performance if I'm currently getting good evaluations? As the external environment changes, the quality of their execution stays the same. They are standing still on that aforementioned, ever-descending escalator.

Studer Group has done a lot of research in this area. Figure 3.2 shows the goals one organization set in year one. Clearly, they did not achieve the desired results.

Year 1 - Goals

Issue	Reduce Costs/ Improve Financial Performance	Provider of Choice (Patient Satisfaction)	Employer of Choice (Employee Satisfaction)
Goals	Achieve financial margins of: - 4.0% in FY '06 - YTD 4.6% more detail> - 5.0% in FY '07 ☺	Achieve organization-wide average patient satisfaction scores of: - 93.7 for "Overall quality of care/ services" - YTD 93.5 ☹ - 76.1 for "Would you recommend" - YTD 73.5 ☹	Reduce overall turn-over of: - "permanent" posi-tions to 11% - YTD 14% ☹ more detail> - "permanent" core RN positions to 13% - YTD 16% ☹

Issue	Improve Care (Quality, Safety, Effectiveness)	Information Management
Goals	Achieve 90% compliance with CMS measures: Community Acquired Pneumonia 3>90% - 5<90% ☹ Surgical Infection Prevention 1>90% - 2<90% ☹ Heart Failure 2>90% - 2<90% ☹ Acute Myocardial Infarction 5>90% - 2<90% ☹ Achieve 90% compliance with evidence-based practice for prophylaxis of the following: DVT/PE, Post-op UTI, Post-op Pneumonia, Post-op AMI, Pressure Sores, Post-op Sepsis	- Implement Employee Satisfaction Assessment process during 2005 - Create projected timeline for the implementation of the Advanced Point of Care (APOC) clinical system

StuderGroup▼
© 2009

Figure 3.2: Organization Example - Year 1 Goals and Results

In fact, out of their nine goals they achieved only one. This is not to say their performance was terrible in the other areas. In fact, some of the performance results they were dissatisfied with would actually be considered good elsewhere. However, this particular organization had pretty high standards.

The Disconnect Between Great Evaluations and Not-So-Great Results

After reviewing these results, we examined their leader evaluations and the results were quite interesting. (By the way, I recommend you do the same. Ask the HR department to take the evaluation tool you are currently using and compare last year's results with the "goal" categories you're using.) There may be a disconnect between these two graphics.

Note that the rating scale this organization uses consists of categories titled *substantially exceeds, exceeds, meets,* and *does not meet* (expectations). As you can see, 73.8 percent of the leaders in this organization fall into the *substantially exceeds* category.

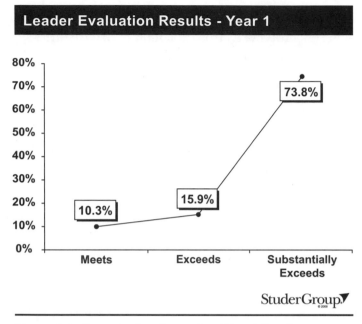

Figure 3.3: Organization Example – Year 1 Leader Evaluation Distribution

How can this be? How is it that most of an organization's leaders can receive a "substantially exceeds" rating in their annual evaluations, when in the same year the organization hit only one of its nine goals? If a leader's performance substantially exceeds expectations, shouldn't the organization's results *also* substantially exceed expectations?

Healthcare organizations are using ineffective evaluation tools—or if they *are* using effective tools, they're falling short on the execution. One of the biggest problems is the use of subjective evaluation tools. It's important that we grade our leaders objectively, not subjectively—on performance rather than personality, in other words.

Many organizations spend more time and money determining what their logo looks like and what message goes under it than on implementing a good evaluation tool!

> The best organizations have leaders who are not afraid to be held accountable, who welcome having their performance measured accurately. This is something that cannot be delegated. The CEO has to take the lead in creating a culture of accountability. And he or she can learn a lot by observing the practices of a particular colleague: the CFO.

What We Can Learn from CFOs

I believe chief financial officers are some of the best leaders in healthcare. They are a good group to learn from.

I got a very close look at how many CFOs operate during the three years when I was a board member for the Healthcare Financial Management Association. (I am extremely impressed with this organization and its members.)

You may have noticed that the CFO sometimes gets a bad rap. In fact, he is sometimes accused of being a "bean counter" or (if people are in a very bad mood) even a penny pincher. This is completely unfair, of course. CFOs are extremely important. Their focus on finances allows the organization to keep its doors open to patients and, of course, keeps huge numbers of people employed!

I have tremendous respect for all kinds of leaders and I believe the majority of them do a very tough job well. We all have different strengths and we can all learn certain valuable lessons from each other.

I happen to believe that in the area of accountability, CFOs generally do an exceptional job. Here's why:

1) CFOs and their direct reports have very specific goals. When I've asked a CFO what his goal in accounts receivable is, for instance, I have never heard, "to become aware of or to increase understanding of...nurses on hourly rounding." A CFO would say to reduce falls. All leaders can adopt the CFO's preference for precision rather than fuzziness.

2) CFOs really measure the data. They have a specific way to measure performance and they don't question the method of measurement. In other healthcare arenas when leaders don't like the data (on productivity, for instance), they may start asking questions: *Who else has been benchmarked? What were they? How many floors did they have? Where are they located?* Finance people don't rationalize. They accept the measurement tool as is.

3) CFOs keep a close watch on variance. I have asked financial officers around the country how many days of cash collections they must fall behind before they start taking action. ("Action" may just mean asking

some questions and digging deeper.) Their answer is nearly always "three to five days."

Yes, CFOs know what's going on at all times and they know what the limits are. Ask one how long someone in the organization could get away with poor expense management before the Finance Department would take action, and his response is usually "from three days to maybe six months at the most."

Ask yourself: *In most organizations, how many years can a department have high staff turnover before its manager is held accountable? How long can it go along "business as usual" with its patient satisfaction score falling short of its goal?*

Recently, I was in an organization and I looked back at its last three years. During that time the patient satisfaction scores for the Emergency Department ranged anywhere from the 4th to the 25th percentile. The ED is the biggest word of mouth department for the hospital. Its highest score was only in the 25th percentile. Yet the senior leadership team continued to keep the same physician group—some of the same players.

Why?

> If expenses go through the roof, senior leaders don't wait years to make changes. So why don't we treat service, quality, and people in the same way that we treat dollars?

For more insights from Quint Studer on what leaders can learn from CFOs, please visit www.studergroup.com/StraightALeadership.

How to Analyze Evaluation Results

Earlier, we looked at an organization's year-one results. Now, let's look at their results from a year later, after they've implemented an objective evaluation tool. Notice that they've grouped their goals under the Five Pillars of Excellence, a model that Studer Group recommends our clients adopt in order to help them get aligned in regard to setting organizational goals. Notice, also, they had a better operational performance than ever before.

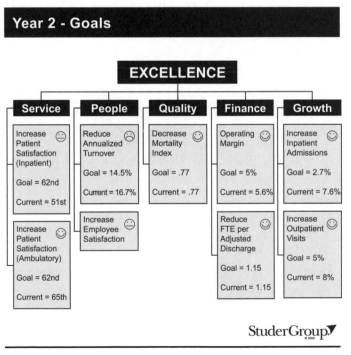

Figure 3.4: Organization Example - Year 2 Goals and Results

Notice that this particular organization's evaluation looks like a Bell Curve. This is not always the case, of course. The higher an organization performs, the more leaders will have high 3s and 4s and be pushed into the upper echelon. The worst performing organizations should have more 2s and 1s.

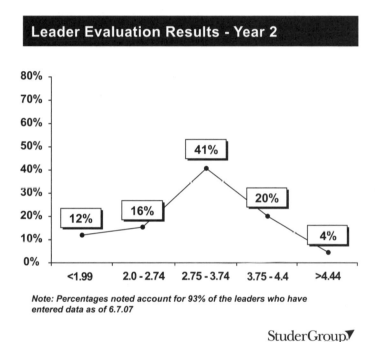

Figure 3.5: Organization Example – Year 2 Leader Evaluation Distribution

Here, about 24 percent of their leaders are exceeding goals, with scores of 3.75 or above, and would be considered high performers. Forty-one percent are meeting their goals (2.75-3.74) and would be strong middle performers. Sixteen percent are achieving some goals (2.0-2.74) but obviously not achieving others, so would be categorized as low middle performers. We assume with strong development they could move into the middle performing category.

That leaves 12 percent of leaders with low performance scores (less than 1.99). This 12 percent is deeply concerning. These are individuals who need to hold up the mirror on their own performance. They absolutely will have to change their performance, their techniques, and their behaviors if they want to perform better and move into that middle row. Note that these are the same leaders who were evaluated favorably a year ago! Every one of those low performing leaders was told that he/she either met, exceeded, or substantially exceeded his/her goals the year before.

Obviously, ineffective evaluations harm organizations financially, sometimes in hard-to-measure ways. When we fail to give leaders a fair and honest score, we cheat the organization out of whatever bottom-line increases might have resulted from their efforts to improve their performance before the next evaluation. Who can ever know what might have been?

Priorities Change. Fast. (Can Your Evaluation Tool Keep Up?)

Weighting each leader's evaluation goals helps her prioritize. (See Chapter 15.) Yet, the priority you set one year might not be the priority you set the next year. We have seen organizations close the evaluation at the end of three to six months and say, "Here's your evaluation score for this part of the year. We're going to modify the weights of the metrics based on changes in the external environment."

When the external environment changes, it does not change perfectly in sync with budget time. It's possible for leaders to achieve their goals but not hit their bottom-line goal because of a change in the external environment.

To adapt to a changing external environment, leaders must make sure they have an evaluation tool that gets them there. Ninety percent or more of the evaluation tools that we see don't fall into that category. That's why when we work with an organization we usually say: "In order for us to be successful, we'd like to make sure that you use our evaluation tool or one that we feel will work."

They usually say right away, "No, we're not comfortable with the tool we're using now, and in fact, we haven't liked it forever." Just be careful: There are a lot of providers putting a lot of bells-and-whistles evaluation tools out there. And these tools generally don't help organizations succeed.

> Remember, the point is not to please everyone. The goal is not to have the sexiest evaluation tool in the world. The best leadership evaluation tool is one that allows you to drive results. How fancy it is doesn't matter. How effective it is *does*.

If your leaders are doing what they're supposed to be doing and if you're seeing consistently improving outcomes, you've probably got the right tool in place. (It may also be due to your leadership. Ask yourself: *Are systems in place to sustain the game when I am not there?*) And that means your foundation for Straight A Leadership is complete. Congratulations…you're well on your way to creating an organization that's a great place for employees to work, physicians to practice medicine, and patients to receive care.

To learn more about the subject of accountability, visit www.studergroup.com/StraightALeadership.

SUMMARY

Accountability is the third "A" of leadership. It does matter how well aligned an organization's leaders are or even whether they have the right skill sets if they aren't being held accountable for their actions. Accountability is the glue that holds the best laid plans together.

When Studer Group does its organizational assessment, we ask, *How well does your current leader evaluation system hold people accountable?* The majority of respondents answer with a lukewarm *fair*.

Further probing usually confirms our suspicions that leaders aren't being held accountable. In most organizations, the majority of leaders are given "substantially exceeds expectations" ratings on their evaluations. However, when we look at how well that same organization is meeting its yearly goals, the results don't match up with these glowing reviews. There's a serious disconnect!

CEOs need to take the lead in creating accountable cultures. They need to approach accountability like CFOs do: by setting very specific goals, properly measuring the data, and keeping a close watch on variances.

Finally, know that priorities can change on a dime, depending on what's happening in the external environment. Make sure your evaluation system allows you to adjust leader priorities as often, and as quickly, as needed.

CHAPTER FOUR:

LEADER CONSISTENCY & BEST PRACTICES

Healthcare leaders believe in consistency. As an industry, we have lots of rules on making things consistent throughout the organization. Physicians, nurses, and other professionals follow the basic core procedures. Organizations standardize which brands of supplies are bought, how patients are admitted, and the temperature at which the food is served. They even insist that our organization's logo and tagline must be used a certain way anywhere it appears.

So you'd think the most important aspect of all— leadership quality—would be highly consistent, right? Well, sure, you'd think so. But the reality is quite different.

The next item in Studer Group's organizational assessment is as follows: *Rate your perception of the consistency in leadership throughout the organization.* Participants choose a number from 1 to 10, with 1 being "Worst" and 10 being "Best in Class."

Organizational Assessment

Rate your perception of the consistency in leadership throughout the organization.

(1=Worst to 10=Best in Class)

		Worst								Best in Class	
		1	2	3	4	5	6	7	8	9	10
Senior Leader	5.95	0	1	1	4	11	7	10	7	0	0
Department Director	6.05	1	2	7	15	37	21	36	16	11	2
Manager	6.07	2	8	13	24	63	57	67	51	12	2
Other	6.24	0	0	0	2	5	3	3	3	0	1
Total	6.08	3	11	21	45	106	88	116	77	23	5

StuderGroup▼

Figure 4.1: Organizational Assessment – Consistency of Leadership

Only a small percentage of respondents in the assessment represented by the above graphic rated their organization a 9 or a 10 for an average score of approximately 6.0 in leadership consistency. And this organization is not unusual.

Think about your own organization. Some departments consistently get better results than others, right? And maybe certain departments get great results during the week but not on the weekend...or during the day but not at night.

Why? Inconsistent leadership.

Organizations that have leaders who behave inconsistently simply can't be aligned. It's possible that all the leaders understand the external environment and all are committed to the same goals—but if they're not practicing the same tactics, none of that matters. They won't be able to get to the next level of performance, and if by some chance they do, they won't be able to sustain it.

On the other hand, healthcare organizations with consistently excellent leadership tend to thrive. They have uniformly positive clinical outcomes. They have high patient, physician, and staff satisfaction scores. They have low staff turnover. They have a culture that attracts the best, the brightest, and the most passionate healthcare professionals in the field.

So where does all this lead us? Inevitably, it leads us to the question of what leaders *should* be doing consistently...and the answer is "best practices."

Best Practices Are Over-Discussed and Underused.

Healthcare leaders love the concept of best practices. And no wonder. When a particular technique or process is proven to yield a better outcome than any other, it just makes sense to adopt it. "Reinventing the wheel" is never a smart move. I've been traveling the country now for almost 10 years, and I've found best practices in many parts of an organization.

Most organizations have areas of success. What's more, they don't mind sharing them.

We'll go into an organization, see what they are doing effectively, and ask if we can share their practices with others. They quickly agree to share because as a rule healthcare people are very giving. They want patients, no matter where they are, to receive excellent care. But does this attitude translate easily into action? Not always.

> If healthcare professionals were great at adopting others' best practices, every organization would be doing better in hand washing and in preventing infections and falls. We would have fewer no-shows and re-admissions. Throughout the country there are stellar organizations that do well in all of these categories, but identifying best practices really does not seem to be the problem. The problem is *moving* best practices.

Leaders Are Reluctant to Ask for Help.

Years ago I was in California working with a large organization that provides services to hospitals. Their leaders felt that the more aligned they were with the hospitals they wanted to contract with, the more likely they would be to be selected over their competition. So they asked me to come share my knowledge of hospitals with them from a CEO's perspective.

The first morning I asked the regional president to identify a leader who gets excellent results in the organization. He told me the name of a director. In fact, he remarked that if every one of their managers had similar results, hospitals across the country would be knocking on their door in order to receive services from them.

Before the session I met with this director and complimented her on her results. In true high performer fashion, she downplayed the great job she was doing. She didn't want to come off as being boastful, but the fact remained that based on measurable outcomes, she was doing a truly great job.

There were around 200 leaders at the meeting. I asked the group if they knew which leader in the room had the best results. It was amazing how many people knew exactly who she was.

I had her stand up and congratulated her on her accomplishments. Then I asked her to look around the room. I asked, "How many of these individuals have visited you in the past two years?" She didn't want to answer but I coaxed her to do so. Eventually she said, "None."

Then I asked, "How many of them have called you?" She looked around and said maybe three or four. So out of the 200 people in this room, only three or four had called her, and none had visited her—yet everybody knew she had the best practices.

What's even more amazing is that most of these leaders in the room owned stock in the company. If the company did better, they not only did well in their own job but they profited monetarily. Yet, for some reason, they never tried to learn from this apparently well-known great leader in order to improve the organization.

Organizations Aren't Great at Standardizing and Transferring Best Practices.

This brings me to the next part of Studer Group's organizational assessment. We ask, *How well does your organization move best practices throughout the rest of the organization?* Answers are determined on a scale 1 through 10.

Organizational Assessment

Rate the skill set at your organization in implementing and standardizing best practices throughout the organization.
(1=Worst to 10=Best in Class)

		Worst								Best in Class	
		1	2	3	4	5	6	7	8	9	10
Senior Leader	5.52	0	2	5	4	12	11	9	4	1	0
Physician	6.2	0	1	0	4	6	6	4	7	2	0
Department Director	6.12	1	2	8	19	24	26	39	28	2	4
Manager	6.55	0	3	10	22	53	46	73	69	27	4
Other	6.11	0	0	2	2	3	2	6	3	1	0
Total	6.31	1	8	25	51	98	91	131	111	33	8

StuderGroup▼

Figure 4.2: Organizational Assessment – Implementation of Best Practices

We've learned from Frederick Reichheld, who wrote the book *Loyalty Rules*, that a 1 through 10 scale works better for questions like this, because it creates a better spread. Obviously 9s and 10s are what you really want, because those scores show you've really got the skill you're measuring hardwired. Sixes, 7s, and 8s mean that you're doing okay, but you've got a ways to go. Anything below a 6 means the skill is seldom put into use.

Unfortunately, in healthcare the average score usually lands between a 5 and a 6. We've never had more than 10 percent of the people say they are a 9 or 10. So here we have these excellent individuals achieving best practices in their own departments, yet somehow the transfer of practices, which will make the organization better, is not being achieved to the needed degree.

Typically, even when a best practice is identified, moving it throughout the organization is a huge challenge. Many high performers aren't willing to share their methods, and for a variety of reasons.

The next step is to use focus groups to dig a little deeper into the "why" of this issue. And we've found that there are a number of reasons why organizations have trouble moving best practices.

Eight "Roadblocks" That Keep Us from Moving Best Practices

1) Sometimes high performers go underground. It's almost like they don't want people to know how well they are doing. They minimize what they do. Ask a high-performing organization how it gets great results and leaders might say, "Oh, we don't do anything differently from

our competition." To find out what makes high performers tick, you have to dig deep.

Digging deep with a high performer is how hourly rounding impact was discovered. I asked a nurse manager who her best nurse was, and then I went to the nurses and said, "I'm just curious. Who is really a star nurse here?" They all gave me the same name.

I met up with the star nurse when she came out of a patient's room, and I said, "You know, all of your co-workers think you're excellent. They think you are one of the best nurses they've ever worked with."

She was embarrassed and said, "Oh, we're all good."

I said, "Well, what do you do that makes such a difference?"

She said, "Oh, nothing, nothing."

I wouldn't give up and said, "Well, you must do something."

She said, "Well, I do tell my patients when I'm going to be back. I found out that if I can give them a time I'm going to be back that my call lights rarely go off and the patients seem to appreciate that." (Here, she showed me the sheet that she used to keep up with patient rounding times.)

That is a best practice. In fact, we've been able to move that best practice to many organizations around the country. Those that implement and develop hourly rounding have verified that they have experienced a 50 percent reduction in falls.

In fact, if everyone in healthcare today rounded hourly between 6:00 a.m. and 10:00 p.m., healthcare costs could be reduced by billions of dollars every year due to decreased patient falls.

> **Thus, one reason best practices aren't regularly transferred is because the people who do them are typically reluctant to bring attention to themselves. They are a little sheepish about how good they are and often feel like, "Well, I just do what I do." Their best practice has not been written down or formulated.**

2) The leader fears losing his edge. If he tells everyone about his best practice, he will then be unable to keep up his success. This does not happen frequently, but it does come up.

3) The high-performing leader balks at taking on a "teaching" role. When high-performing leaders are asked to present their best practices to other people in their organization, they are often reluctant. They don't want others in the organization to think that they are showing off or that they are the boss's favorite. And when they do present, they will even give reasons for why they could successfully implement the best practice but it may be hard for others. They minimize what they are doing. They feel uncomfortable being separated from the pack. Often a high-performing leader will do a better job at explaining one of his best practices to another organization than he will teaching it to his own.

4) Success is attributed to the leader and *not* the best practice. Often, the leaders who create and/or implement best practices are high performers in a particular organization, and it is assumed that it is their leadership and not the best practice itself that is getting the great results. When that happens, the actual best practice is missed or underestimated.

5) Leaders want to keep their autonomy. Implementing someone else's way of doing something makes them feel they are giving up this autonomy. It moves them out of their comfort zone. This is especially true in the C-Suite.

6) "Terminal uniqueness" can hamper moving best practices. For some reason healthcare organizations always need to feel different. Leaders are quick to point out how they are just a little bit unique, a little bit different, and that's why a certain best practice won't work at their organization. Of course, this attitude protects them from potential failure.

A leader may worry that if she can't successfully implement this best practice, as her colleague has, that she is not a good leader. She chooses not to implement the best practice, and comes up with a reason why it won't work for her employees. It protects her from fully having to realize, "We can't perform. *I* can't perform."

7) Egos get in the way. By the time some people get to the C-Suite, they are better leaders than followers. Or at least they think they are! When an executive has been giving orders and teaching people how to follow

directives for a long time, it can be difficult for him to copy or duplicate another senior leader or organization.

8) There is too much change and not enough time. For many healthcare organizations, there seems to be a new way of doing something every day of the week. When that happens, there isn't enough time for a new best practice to be mastered. And when it isn't mastered, it won't last, which creates the feeling among employees that the best practice did not live up to expectations. When those desired results aren't achieved, the best practice will be dropped every time.

The Most Successful Leaders Put Their Egos in Their Pockets.

The best leaders in healthcare are the most humble ones. They do not seek personal glory. They put the well-being of their organization ahead of their own ego. Community Health Systems (CHS) in Franklin, Tennessee— a highly successful network of more than 120 hospitals in 29 states—is a good example. When Wayne Smith, Chairman, President & Chief Executive Officer, saw the impact that hourly rounding had on quality, he implemented a system to integrate the practice into every one of their hospitals.

Leaders like those at CHS truly believe, "If this best practice will help me get the results I want, I will implement it." They don't get hung up on who developed the best practice. They remind me a lot of physicians.

Every week I ask the physicians I meet with the same question: "If you read in a respected publication about new research that will lead to better patient outcomes but implementing the results of the research meant adjusting something in your practice, how long would it take you to make the change?" Without fail, they tell me they would implement those changes immediately.

Why? Because a physician's number one goal is a better clinical outcome. Even though something might be uncomfortable to her, she will do it. She won't say, "You know, I'm not going to use this new method because it was developed at Dartmouth, and I'm at Vanderbilt." She doesn't say, "Well, Baylor did it that way, so we're going to do it our own way."

In fact, many of the already very good organizations Studer Group is fortunate enough to work with are always looking for best practices. They don't worry about who gets the credit. Their main focus is getting the best clinical and operational outcomes.

> When people and organizations put their egos in their pockets, when they're able to learn and implement the best practices of others, they will only get better. When they move best practices, they have positive outcomes. And isn't that why we're all here?

Patient and Physician Perceptions Are Critical, Too.

Finally, we ask two more assessment questions: *From a patient/family perspective and point of view, how would a patient/family rate your organization?* and *Rate your perception of the ease of practicing medicine for physicians at your organization.* In both instances, leaders taking the assessment choose a number from 1 to 10, with 1 being "Worst" and 10 being "Best in Class."

Organizational Assessment

From a patient/family perspective and point of view, how would a patient/family rate your organization?
(1=Worst to 10=Best in Class)

		Worst								Best in Class	
		1	2	3	4	5	6	7	8	9	10
Senior Leader	7.33	0	0	0	0	6	2	17	17	5	1
Physician	7.00	0	0	1	0	4	4	8	10	3	0
Department Director	7.35	0	0	0	2	15	20	36	55	21	4
Manager	7.34	0	1	5	5	26	28	84	102	45	11
Other	7.21	0	0	0	0	1	2	11	3	1	1
Total	7.32	0	1	6	7	52	56	156	187	75	17

StuderGroup.▼

Figure 4.3: Organizational Assessment – Patient/Family Perspective

Organizational Assessment

Rate your perception of the ease of practicing medicine for physicians at your organization.
(1=Worst to 10=Best in Class)

		Worst								Best in Class	
		1	2	3	4	5	6	7	8	9	10
Physician	5.9	0	0	2	6	5	5	7	3	1	1

StuderGroup▼

Figure 4.4: Organizational Assessment – Physician Perception

While this book does not cover these questions in detail, I wanted to mention them. We use them to get a sense of how leaders believe the organization is perceived by these two important groups: the people it cares for and its physician partners.

Also, the questions allow us to track improvement as time goes on. When an organization is able to get aligned, take the right actions, hold people accountable, and move best practices, patient and physician satisfaction will almost always increase.

I've found that these two questions help leaders connect to the real reasons we do all this work and strive so hard to improve. It reminds them that these groups (their customers and their partners in healing) play central roles in the reality they're seeking to create—a better place for patients to receive care, for employees to work, and for physicians to practice medicine.

SUMMARY

Most healthcare organizations struggle with leader consistency. One of Studer Group's organizational assessment questions—*Rate your perception of the consistency in leadership throughout the organization*—proves the point.

It's important for leaders to be consistently effective throughout the organization. When they aren't, organizations can't achieve the results they seek. When they are, on the other hand, they create the kind of culture that yields great clinical outcomes, high patient satisfaction, and passionate, dedicated employees.

"Straight A" organizations are ones in which all leaders in every department consistently embrace proven best practices.

It just makes sense to adopt and implement best practices—it's far more effective than trying to "reinvent the wheel." And healthcare professionals are usually eager to share their best practices with others. What they're not so great at is asking for guidance themselves, even from a "superstar" who works in their own organization.

Many healthcare organizations struggle with moving best practices. The next question on our organizational assessment—*Rate the skill set at your organization in implementing and standardizing best practices throughout the organization*—usually yields an average score of between 5 and 6 (out of a possible 10).

Why is it so tough for organizations to move best practices? There are many possible reasons. Often, high performers are reluctant to talk about what makes them so successful. They don't like the attention. They don't want to be viewed as thinking they're "better" than everyone else. Or perhaps they may fear losing their recognition as "the best" if they share their secret. Other leaders may fear losing their autonomy if they adopt a new way of doing things, or failing at the implementation. Sometimes ego won't let them be followers.

A great leader never lets ego prevent him or her from embracing someone else's better idea. Remember, moving best practices yields better outcomes. By improving the implementation of best practices, consistency also naturally improves.

Next, we ask two final questions: *From a patient/family perspective and point of view, how would a patient/family rate your organization?* and *Rate your perception of the ease of practicing medicine for physicians at your organization.*

These questions allow us to get a sense of how leaders see these two important groups as perceiving the organization and to track improvement as time goes on. They also remind leaders of the central role these two groups play in creating a world-class organization—one that's a better place for patients to receive care, for employees to work, and for physicians to practice medicine.

SECTION TWO:

EXTERNAL ENVIRONMENT COMMUNICATION TOOLS

O nce senior leaders are aligned in their view of the external environment and its implications, they must make sure the rest of the organization is, too. Not only must mid-level leaders be on the same page as senior leaders, so should all employees under *them*.

In this section we'll outline some practical ways to close the gap between senior leaders and everyone else. Chances are you're already using most of these communication tools. Now you're about to discover how they can help you integrate information about the external environment into your daily operations.

Section 2 covers:
- Senior Leader Visibility
- Tough Questions
- Financial Impact Grid
- Meeting Model
- Rounding
- Standards of Behavior

- Employee Forums
- Communication Boards
- Newsletters

Utilized properly, these tools and tactics can help ensure that everyone in your organization knows the challenges faced by your organization. They'll go a long way toward getting everyone aligned, taking the right actions, and holding each other (and themselves!) accountable for the results.

CHAPTER FIVE TOOL:

SENIOR LEADER VISIBILITY

P eople often ask me about senior leader visibility. *How important is it for senior leaders to be seen and heard through-out the organization?* they ask. *Should senior leaders round on staff? And what should be the purpose of that rounding?*

I tell them that yes, senior leaders *should* do a certain amount of rounding on staff. Particularly when a tough external environment is shaking things up, the physical presence of the CEO and other C-Suite executives can be reassuring. But senior leader rounding can be over-rated.

Obviously, this doesn't mean that when a senior lead-er is walking down the hall that he is not going to say hello or that he shouldn't stop to talk to staff. Better lead-ers make themselves visible whenever they can. But it's mostly important for them to round on their direct re-ports.

(Now, please don't read this and think, *Well he's just saying that so C-Suite leaders don't have to leave their offices. He's just catering to them since they hire him!*)

Research shows the key to success in any department is the direct supervisor. They are the ones running day-to-day operations in the department, so it's more important that *they* are more visible to employees than senior leaders.

When senior leaders do round inside departments, they need to really make their time count. That means they need to practice not just rounding, but strategic rounding.

Strategic Rounding and the External Environment

> Strategic rounding is centered on preparation. Before senior leaders round on employees inside a particular department, they need to do their homework so that the visit is as effective and efficient as possible and they get the most bang for their rounding buck.

It's important that they organize their thoughts on the external environment and how it's affecting the organization. They need to prepare themselves to answer any tough questions employees might toss their way. And they need to be ready to proactively address any specific impact the external environment has had on that particular department.

If you're the CEO (or other senior leader), here's an example of what you might say: "I know last month we had a reduction in force. I know that there are two fewer employees here than there used to be. It was a tough decision to make. Let me again explain how the decision came about. I want to thank you for your focus on making sure things ran well during this adjustment."

Then be specific on actions they took.

Scouting Reports

Of course, the external environment is only one of the subjects you'll address. You'll also want to discuss other issues specific to the department you're rounding in. And the best way to prepare yourself for them is to have the department manager give you a scouting report beforehand.

Scouting reports can be easily compiled from the rounding logs department managers keep. (See Chapter 9.) They are immensely useful tools for helping senior leaders expedite their own rounding process. Here is a sample scouting report:

Senior Leader Scouting Report

Name _____ Department _____

Dept/Person Rounded on _____ Date/Week of _____

Key Words or Questions	Special Employee Issues	
Information - to be completed by department leader in advance of Senior Leader Rounding	**Comments**	
Accomplishments of the Department		
New Equipment Purchased		
Staff to Recognize	Who	What/Why
Current Expense Management Results		
Tough Questions		
External Environment and Industry Issues		
Physician Activities or Issues		
Current Patient Satisfaction Results		
Current Employee Satisfaction Results		

StuderGroup.▼

Figure 5.1: Senior Leader Scouting Report – External Environment

The scouting report provides you with important information about a given department: who you should recognize, what you should do while you're there, and what is going on in general. It helps you answer any questions that keep coming up and give kudos based on how well the department has done in a certain area.

> A good scouting report can help a senior leader recognize the right people in a particular department. It can also help you acknowledge which systems have been fixed and what tools and equipment have been purchased—as well as which ones still need attention. Being able to talk about all this "inside information" will help you get a win with your employees.

Finally, scouting reports can give you a valuable "heads-up" regarding anything out of the ordinary that's going on—so that you won't be ambushed by unexpected information.

A Leadership Lesson from Military History

I recently read a book about George Washington that contained a very interesting anecdote about British General Edward Braddock, who he served under. In a battle, Braddock had a huge, huge military advantage. But when he entered into the French and Indian War, during the Battle of the Monongahela, his troops got demolished, and he was killed. Why? One of the reasons is that his army did not have a scouting report.

General Braddock was not aware of what he was up against. He didn't know that the enemy's fighting style would be different from what he was accustomed to. He didn't know that the terrain was such that the artillery would not even make it to where they were trying to pull it. If he had had a scouting report, I'm not saying he and his troops would have won, but they certainly would have experienced fewer casualties.

I don't mean to compare your organization to a war zone. Everyone has come together to save lives, not take them. Still, when dealing with so many diverse individuals and agendas, problems are bound to crop up from time to time.

Senior leaders, use your scouting reports to prepare yourselves (as much as humanly possible, anyway) for what you might encounter when you do staff rounding. This will help you be as absolutely effective as you can be. Your time and everyone else's is too valuable not to be used wisely.

CHAPTER SIX TOOL:

TOUGH QUESTIONS

W hen you're the leader, people look to you for answers. And sometimes the questions asked can be difficult to answer if one is not prepared. That's especially true when a changing external environment forces the organization to make hard decisions—decisions that can be costly to employees in terms of convenience, money, and sometimes even their jobs.

It's not unusual for a leader to be so blindsided by an employee's tough question that it perpetuates the "we/they" phenomenon. In other words, an answer is given that unintentionally positions someone or the organization in a negative light.

Let's say I am a leader who announces that we are going to cut back on overtime because money is tight. I should be prepared for the tough questions that will follow such a statement. For instance: *Where is the organization getting the money for the new construction project that's going on... or the lobby that was just redecorated...or the outside consultant brought in to do leadership training? Why wasn't that money spent on the patient care room, which seemed to need it more?*

> The way leaders make money decisions can be very confusing for employees. After all, staff don't have all of the data. But when a person is prepared for those questions—and has a good answer at the ready—an uncomfortable conversation can be turned into an educational and highly productive one.

The Tough Questions Exercise

What's the Tough Questions Exercise? It's a technique used to teach leaders across the country how to prepare for and respond to those tough questions.

Step 1 is capturing the questions. At the next department meeting have leaders bring in the questions they are hearing from employees and physicians. Do not judge why someone did not better answer a particular question, even if the one they provide is upsetting. If you go into "judging" mode, you will shut down the leaders.

Chances are, leaders *will* bring questions that you will be surprised they can't answer. Realize early on the goal is simply to harvest the questions even if they are along the lines of: *Why can't we have more staff?* or *Why did Department A get this and Department B did not?*

There will be tough questions resulting from the external environment. For example, questions like, *Is there going to be a reduction in force? Are we going to eliminate some services? Are we going to slow down our building campaign? Are we still going to get pay raises? What's this going to do to our benefits? Are any senior leader positions going to be eliminated?"*

The best way to handle these questions is to be factual and transparent. People appreciate these qualities, especially people who work in healthcare. Remember, employees must tell patients some difficult things and deliver some of the toughest messages in the world. Healthcare leaders must also be prepared to deliver tough messages and answer the tough questions from employees and physicians.

Questioning the Questioner

After a list of the harvested tough questions has been completed, have some fun. Break the leaders into teams and assign each team a question. For example: *So...are we going to get more staff?*

Ask the leaders in that team to reveal how they would handle the question. Instead of just saying yes or no, leaders too may say, "If it were up to me, you would get more staff, but you know how the administration is." (A perfect example of we/they!)

Instead, teach leaders to say, "Well, tell me exactly why you feel you need more staff." Likewise, if somebody asks about a piece of equipment, the leader would ask, "If you had that piece of equipment, how would it help you do your job better?"

People tend to provide a general answer when doing a little digging will yield the information to form a much better response. Questioning the questioner won't necessarily ensure an answer of "yes." What it *will* do is help the leader to know what is behind the question so that she can provide a better diagnosis of the problem.

The leader may well discover that the issue that sparked the question is a situational one. In other words, the perceived shortage of staff or need for a new piece of equipment is a temporary problem that doesn't require a permanent solution.

It takes discipline to probe for the deeper issue rather than responding with an off-the-cuff answer. The Tough Questions Exercise helps a team practice this art.

Aligned Answers Equal Aligned Organizations.

Think about what would happen if an employee asked every leader at the organization the same question. Would he get the same response from all of them? In the end that is the goal. And it is extremely important that one organization runs better, not one organization for every leader.

Many times when I'm in an organization and ask a group, "If you have 300 leaders and 300 leaders get the same question, how many different answers will you have?" The answer is usually, "300." Ideally, it would be "one." Why? Because one answer would mean you were aligning messages and resources across your organization.

An important goal of the Tough Questions Exercise is to teach leaders the "preferred answer" to any given question.

After you collect these questions, compile them, answer them, and send them out to all the employees. Tell them that their leadership team collected the content and dubbed it the organization's "tough questions." This exercise also identifies the skills and information leaders must have to be successful in their challenging interactions.

Ask leaders to review these tough questions at their next department meeting. Doing so will allow them to open the floor for new questions and to ensure that everybody understands the answers that were given for the questions.

When rounding, bring up these questions to evaluate if the leaders have been addressing these items—items that if not dealt with impede efficient and effective operations.

Ultimately, what you want to do is identify the challenges that arise due to changes in the external environment, and then align your resources to solve them. The first resource happens to be human capital. Leaders' ability to answer the tough questions is vital for a strong, well-aligned organization.

Tough Question Exercise

Goal: Developing Better Leaders - Helping leaders have answers to the tough questions

Exercise Instructions: Using an identified tough question, use this worksheet to work through to identify key words to use to best answer the question and further learning and consistency in your organization.

The Tough Question:

1. What questions should you ask to further understand the employee's question?
   a. _____
   b. _____
   c. _____

2. What is the underlying issue or issues?
   a. _____
   b. _____

3. What is your best response to the employee's question or issue?
   _____
   _____
   _____

4. What skills and information do you need to deal with this question?
   _____
   _____
   _____

StuderGroup▼

Figure 6.1: Tough Question Exercise

CHAPTER SEVEN TOOL:

THE FINANCIAL
IMPACT GRID

W hen financial challenges arise, it is natural for organizations to get anxious. *Very* anxious. We begin to examine every area of our operations to see where we might save dollars or boost revenue. And for most of us, perceived "soft" issues (as opposed to "hard" issues that more obviously relate to the financial bottom line) inevitably come under greater scrutiny.

Our world has changed so much. Back in 1993 patient satisfaction was called "soft." I get frustrated because sometimes people will call the Hospital Consumer Assessment of Healthcare Providers and Systems survey a "patient satisfaction survey"—it is much more.

Normally, by the way, organizations that don't do that well on the HCAHPS survey downplay it by saying, "But we really have good clinical quality." However, the HCAHPS survey measures the patient's perception of quality of care, which includes pain management. How can anyone say managing pain is "soft"?

"Soft" Issues Translate to Cold Hard Cash.

Most people visit a healthcare provider to get help managing pain, to be aware of the side effects of medication, to receive a good understanding of home care instructions, and so forth. They expect (and deserve) to be responded to efficiently and effectively. If they're not, they will go elsewhere the next time they have a medical need and will tell everyone they know to do the same. And they may litigate.

When an organization improves patient perception of care, the likelihood of litigation decreases. Obviously, less litigation equals a positive financial impact.

> Dr. Gerald Hickson of Vanderbilt shows that malpractice suits are tied to complaints. A small percentage of physicians receive 50 percent of the complaints in the healthcare environment, and 5 percent of the physicians have over 90 percent of the lawsuits. And certainly lawsuits are not soft!

Employee turnover is another issue that some may consider soft—yet it strongly impacts clinical care. According to the Voluntary Hospital Association, if employee turnover is below 12 percent, the organization's mortality index is much lower and length of stay is shorter than those that have over 12 percent turnover. Low staff turnover saves lives.

The Financial Impact Grid

It's important that leaders, managers, and employees alike understand exactly how issues traditionally considered "soft" translate to hard financial numbers. To also understand the true cost of medical events; for instance, that every decubitus (bedsore) costs an extra $15,000 in expenses per patient. To see which tools and techniques affect these factors.

The financial impact grid was developed for all of these reasons.

This tool helps leaders "connect the dots" to the financial impact when improvements are made. The grid makes it easy to see where the external environment impacts a financial number such as length of stay. If reimbursement goes down, then leaders at an organization know they need to be more effective and efficient than ever.

The grid also shows the financial impact of implementing tools and techniques aimed at reducing negative metrics and increasing positive ones.

> Let's say leaders know that every fall costs an organization an average of $11,000 in expenses. And then, you pull out the grid and show them there's proof that if leaders round every hour, falls are reduced by 50 percent. In fact, at one New York City hospital alone, hourly rounding accounted for $1.4 million per year in reduced expenses. After learning this, why *wouldn't* they make rounding a priority?

Of Course, It's Not *All* About Money.

Employees will appreciate the fact that certain tools and techniques help reduce expenses, but they will also be excited because they know there is more to a fall, for example, than dollar signs.

After all, they see the patient's pain. They see a family come in, aghast because their sick mother is lying on the floor when they felt they had left her with a healthcare provider they could trust. They also see an anxious family who are now afraid to leave the hospital because their mother might fall again.

So yes, mention the financial impact, but also focus on the human side of the issue. Show people how a certain behavior can improve the organization's bottom line *and* connect it back to purpose, worthwhile work, and making a difference.

Financial Impact Grid

PILLAR	ROI / ECONOMIC LINKAGE	BASELINE	PERIOD 1	PERIOD 2	PERIOD 3
Service	Risk Mgmt File Openings				
	Rick Mgmt File Expenditures				
	Legal Fees				
	Executive Man-hours Spent on Litigation				
Quality	Length of Stay				
	Re-admits				
	Returns to Surgery w/in 48 hours				
	Returns to ED w/in 48 hours				
	No-show Rate				
	Nosocomial Infections				
	Pressure Ulcers				
	Falls				
	Medication Errors				
	Aspirin w/in 2 hours of AMI				
	ED Door to Doc Time				
	Patients Leaving AMA				
	Antibiotics w/in 4 hrs of Pneumonia				
People	Employee Turnover				
	RN Turnover				
	90-Day Turnover				
	Agency Expense				
	PRN Expense				
	Overtime Expense				
	Recruitment Expense				
	Processing Fees				
	Sign-on Incentives				
	Orientation				
Finance	Collections				
	Staff Productivity				
	OR Start Times				
	AR Days				
	ED Left Without Being Seen				
	Diversion Hours in ED				
	Advertising Costs				
Growth	Inpatient Admissions				
	Inpatient Revenue				
	Outpatient Visits				
	ED Volume				
	Outpatient Revenue				
	Surgery Cases				
	Surgery Revenue				
	Consults				
	Market Share				
	Revenue per Physician				
	Revenue per Top 20 Admitters				
	Physician Turnover				
Community	Charitable Giving				
	Volunteer Hours				

StuderGroup▼

Figure 7.1: Financial Impact Grid

CHAPTER EIGHT TOOL:

SUPERVISORY MEETING MODEL

T he external environment drives many of the moves an organization makes. As changes take place outside the organization, corresponding changes must take place *inside* it. And because leaders at all levels implement many of those changes, it's critical that leaders stay in close contact with other leaders they supervise.

That's why supervisory meetings are so critical. I am speaking, of course, of the one-on-one meetings leaders hold with their direct reports. Well-orchestrated, well-designed meetings are the medium through which leaders can consistently convey their changing expectations to the men and women who carry them out. It is also a time of mentoring.

Consistently is the key word in that sentence. One major reason for the existence of these meetings is to standardize practices in order to make the organization operate better. Right? Yet we often see that, ironically, the supervisory meetings themselves are not standardized. They are quite inconsistent in terms of how often they're held and what happens in them.

Inconsistent Meetings Equal Inconsistent Organizations.

I attended a meeting with regional executives from a national company and asked the participants how many direct reports they each had. They said they each had between eight and ten. Then I asked them how often they met with each one. Some said they met every two weeks; some said at least once a month. Some said they met only as needed. Here we see the first steps of inconsistency.

Then I asked what their agendas for these meetings looked like. Based on their answers, I knew that if every executive were to give me the written meeting guidelines he or she used, I'd be holding a handful of agendas that looked nothing alike. See the problem? If the organization is to be aligned, so too must be the agendas for supervisory meetings.

> Think of supervisory meetings as rehearsals for a play or timeouts during a game. You can't align the actors and actresses if everyone shows up at different times and if they all have different scripts. Likewise, in sports it's hard to make adjustments without calling a timeout.

We recommend that leaders adopt the same standardized meeting model and use it for every supervisory meeting held. A sample model follows:

A Meeting Model That Works

Studer Group Supervisory Meeting Model

Leaders bring the following items and results to their immediate supervisor:

1. Leader Evaluation
2. Monthly Report Card
3. *External Environment / Industry Issues*
4. 90-Day Work Plan
5. Linkage Grid from Leadership Development Institute (follow-up assignments)
6. Rounding Logs
7. Thank-You Notes
8. People Trends and Issues - Standards of Behavior

StuderGroup▼

Figure 8.1: Studer Group® Supervisory Meeting Model

Of course, organizations choose to modify this model or create their own. That's fine. Just be sure that every leader uses the same one, then cascade the template to all supervisory sessions. Organizations that have a standard meeting model perform better than those that do not.

Let's say the VP of Operations is holding a supervisory meeting with the director of the Laboratory. The meeting starts with a review of the leader evaluation. This will give a "snapshot" of the yearly goals (desired outcomes). Then, progress to date discussed. This will tell where reward and recognition is needed and will help identify any gaps in performance, which leads to skill development.

If the organization does 90-day plans, pull this up to see what is currently being focused on. If the leaders complete rounding logs (which we highly recommend, by the way), review these documents. Make sure the leader is noting people to recognize, systems that work well, systems that could work better, departments that are doing a nice job, and, tools and equipment that need attention.

> Ask a few other important questions. Are there any particular employees to reach out to, either verbally or with a thank-you note? Are there staff performance concerns? Remember, if you don't ask about performance issues, they will probably get much worse before they surface. By mentioning them in the supervisory meeting, the leader gives others an opportunity to bring them to attention early on, and work on solutions before they turn into chronic problems.

Include a Discussion on the External Environment.

The realities of the external environment permeate every aspect of the supervisory meeting. However, it's important to include the subject as a separate item on the agenda. You might talk about an article you asked the director to read. Instigate a discussion on how the external environment is impacting the organization as a whole and the director's department in particular. And always, always ask about solutions. Department leaders are close to their field. Ask about developments in technology, new unit practices, and so forth that will impact the area.

The whole purpose of this book is to help leaders bring awareness of the external environment to the organization and align resources to deal with it. You want to bring the issue to light at every opportunity, and including it in the meeting model is a good way to do that. And after all, doesn't the external environment influence results, which impact the leader's evaluation, what's included in the 90-day plan, what actions are being taken every month, and whom to recognize?

The changes that are occurring all around the organization certainly affect employee performance—and not always for the better. Yet if people have always gotten good performance reviews prior to a change, they naturally assume they'll continue to get them. This meeting model lets the leader know that, thanks to changes occurring in the external environment, the department can no longer maintain the status quo without sliding into a "low performance" category.

> As leaders, we owe it to the organization, those we serve, and those we supervise to provide consistent mentoring, feedback, and review of their work. The biggest impact a leader has unfolds through the development of others. The best meeting model is the one that helps you maximize that impact.

CHAPTER NINE TOOL:

ROUNDING FOR EXTERNAL ENVIRONMENT ISSUES

L eader rounding has become something of a mainstay for healthcare organizations. The practice was inspired, of course, by the traditional daily rounds physicians make to check on patients. Once other (non-physician) leaders realized the benefits of rounding on staff members, the concept really took off. Today there probably isn't a hospital or a healthcare facility in the country that is *not* doing some type of rounding.

Basic rounding helps leaders meet certain standard goals: making sure that the staff know they are cared about, know what is going on (what's working well, who should be recognized, which systems need to work better, which tools and equipment need attention), and that proper follow-up actions are taking place.

A technique to yield even more powerful results is to build an "external environment" component into the organization's rounding.

First, Prepare the Managers.

Ask managers to think about how they can incorporate the external environment into their rounds. Has there been a story in the paper or a local or national event they want to bring up with the staff? Are there other factors that have been going on in the organization's competitive front that should be brought up while they are rounding?

Don't forget to ask managers what questions *they* may have about the external environment. Harvesting questions helps you figure out where the information shortfalls are and allows you to share consistent answers with all of your managers. That way, they will be prepared to give employees who happen to ask the same questions a standardized, "official" answer.

Make sure managers have the tools to not only discuss the external environment, but also to talk about what the organization is doing to respond to it—and what they, the individuals being rounded upon, should do as well.

> When leaders take the time to explain the external environment and share what they are doing to counteract any problems, it builds tremendous confidence in employees. It shows that the C-Suite is on top of things and promotes the feeling that everyone is working together to solve the issues.

Rounding Reduces Anxiety and Clears up Confusion.

Rounding is a critical tool for organizations seeking to both educate people on the external environment and harvest any concerns or anxieties they might have. Employees read and hear a lot of information, and some of it is very confusing. Rounding helps clear up much of that confusion.

For example, employees might be hearing that healthcare is a huge growth industry and that if someone wants a job all she has to do is go into healthcare. On the other hand, they are also hearing that their organization needs a reduction in force. They may then assume that their organization is not run as well as the ones that are growing. Naturally, that's often not the case.

Take time to round on people who are definitely secure and those who are not so secure, and be open with all groups. For example, if a nurse has been with the organization 22 years, has great seniority, and is highly skilled, the chance of this nurse being let go is probably slim to none. This nurse needs to know that. However, in the case of brand new employees, it is only ethical to let them know where they would stand if reductions were to take place.

Also during rounding, take the time to discuss what can be done to lower or eliminate the possibility of reductions. And don't assume the answer has to be provided. Remember the lesson of Park Ranger Leadership—it's often better for staff to come up with solutions themselves.

Rounding Helps Us Solve Problems.

When I was president of Baptist Hospital, Inc., in Pensacola, Florida, people in the Radiology Department were being sent home early due to less patient volume than budgeted. During rounding, some of those employees said they didn't like working so few hours. The leaders asked them, "What can be done so you won't need to be sent home early?"

They came up with solutions. Employees agreed they could treat doctors much better so they would bring their patients to the Radiology Department. They could treat patients much better so word of mouth would increase. They could call patients before an appointment to reduce no-shows, and they could call people at home after an appointment to make sure the service was great.

A Word about Accountability

Rounding is an incredibly valuable tool when it's done properly. That means not just going through the motions but actually capturing and analyzing what is learned. Make sure rounding logs are used to record any issues raised during these conversations. Getting it down on paper creates accountability for taking necessary actions.

The good news is that within six months no one was being sent home early. Those techniques worked so well that the only complaints received were that people felt they were working too many hours and too much overtime and wanted more time off. And of course, in healthcare you'd rather have complaints about growth than complaints about shrinkage!

So, rounding becomes a key technique for making sure people understand the external environment—and their role in responding to it.

Leader Rounding on Staff Log

Name_____ Department/Unit_____
Employee(s) Rounded on _____ Date/Week of _____

Question related to Absenteeism:	Question related to Safety:
Are there any barriers that we could remove that would help co-workers from calling in sick?	Is there anything that you're aware of that you would consider unsafe, that I should know about?

Steps	Comments	
Personal Connection		
What's working well?		
Is there anyone I should recognize for doing great work?	Who	What/Why
Are there any physicians or other departments that I should recognize?	Who	What/Why
Are there any systems that need improvement?		
Do you have the basic tools and equipment to do your job?		
Tough Questions		
External Environment/Industry Issues, Articles or Topics:		
Behaviors Coached □ AIDET/Key Words □ Customer Service Priorities □ Standards □ Others: _____		
Is there anything I can help you with right now? Thank you for making a difference!		

Review findings with next level leader in one-on-one meetings.

StuderGroup▼
© 2008

Figure 9.1: Leader Rounding on Staff Log

CHAPTER TEN TOOL:

STANDARDS OF BEHAVIOR

B ehavior is always important. After all, the face all staff members present to the world—i.e., to patients, to visitors, to vendors, to the community, and to each other—is what an organization will be judged by. But in times of turmoil, how we behave is even more important.

When big changes are taking place in the external environment, people are most likely under considerable stress. That stress may well impact how we act toward patients, coworkers, and others, and how questions are answered.

Imagine, for instance, that a patient says to someone, "I heard your hospital is in financial trouble. Is that true?" Or a vendor asks, "Aren't you worried about that big outpatient center your competitor is opening?" Or a coworker says, "I heard 25 percent of our staff is going to be laid off. Did you hear that?"

A patient might ask why there are so few nurses. Why? Because they heard the staff say there was a nursing shortage. Or there was a story in the news about a nursing shortage. Or maybe the department really is short-staffed that day.

It's important that everyone is aligned for consistent behavior in a variety of circumstances. Good Standards of Behavior can ensure that.

Be Sure Standards Address the External Environment.

Most organizations have Standards of Behavior guidelines in place already. (Sometimes they're called "Standards of Performance.") Over the last 10 years, such standards have become popular, and the concept has evolved into something of a buzzword.

Typically, the standards cover everything from how staff dress to how to treat coworkers to how to answer the phone to what is (and isn't) okay to say to patients and visitors. They are tremendously valuable in creating a consistent organization. When they're followed (more on this shortly), they provide a welcome sense of stability and normalcy when the external environment is shaking things up.

Standards of Behavior can help employees make sense of and respond to critical changes in the external environment. They can help employees eschew gossip (yes, that can be one of the standards!), speak in a unified voice, and address any tough questions that others might ask with confidence and consistency.

That said, it's important to review standards often to make sure they are still relevant in light of any major changes that may have occurred. And do not hesitate to add new standards when it seems appropriate and necessary.

Are Standards Being Enforced?

Typically, organizations take great care in writing their Standards of Behavior. The employees get together and create the standards. Then, the organization publishes them in a book. The Standards Team feels good. A big show is made of signing the contract. Many times the senior leaders sign it in front of a group of people, which gets everybody excited. The employees sign it. Before new employees are hired, they are asked to sign it.

That's all well and good. But here's the big question: Are people being held accountable to the Standards of Behavior?

There is not a Standards of Behavior contract in existence—and I have read hundreds of them—that would not generate patient satisfaction, employee satisfaction, and physician satisfaction...*if everyone followed it.*

Standards work much like a weight management plan. The plan will tell me what I should (and shouldn't) eat, when I should eat it, and how much of it I should eat. It will tell me to do some exercise, also. If I follow that plan, I will get the desired results. If I don't get the results, then what? Do I go to another plan?

Or do I ask myself, Is the problem the plan…or is the problem me and my behavior?

In healthcare, the problem is usually not the standards. It's the accountability for the standards. To diagnose the organization's accountability, just have Human Resources each month provide the number of employees who have been written up for not following the Standards of Behavior.

Even when your organization is achieving good results, there will be people written up. When I was a hospital president and I did this exercise, I found that 22 percent of employees who were written up were written up for violation of standards. That meant that we were following up, and if people were not meeting the Standards of Behavior, it was being addressed. This was at a time when results were good.

Is your organization doing the same? It's a good idea for leaders to coach the employees at first and to reward and recognize those who do follow the standards—but there comes a time when people who aren't following them should be held accountable. The patients, physicians, and coworkers deserve that.

Check the monthly report on how many people were written up by each department. If certain departments have poor performance but the people are never written up for standard violation, that's a red flag. It means that their leadership is either afraid to hold people accountable or is in need of extra training—or the real issue is the leader. Leaders usually do not hold others to a standard if they are not following it themselves.

Follow Standards or Get Rid of Them.

Ask yourself this question: Do people in your organization see themselves as leaders, or do they see themselves as leaders of their specific department only? (They should see themselves as the former.) If a manager in the organization sees any employee, not just those they supervise, do something that does not meet the Standards of Behavior, will they ignore it or address it? Remember, what we permit, we promote. What we allow, we encourage.

One day I was visiting a hospital in New Jersey. Included in their Standards of Behavior was a requirement that employees say "hi" to visitors if they passed within ten feet of them in the hallway. Another standard required staff to take people to their destination, not just point in its general direction.

While I was talking to a nurse manager, I watched staff pass visitors and not say a word and walk by visitors without offering to take them to where they wanted to go. I asked the leader, "If someone on your staff had a medication error, would you ignore it?" Of course, he said, "Absolutely not. I would address it immediately."

I said, "Well, why is it that all of these people are not following standards and you're not saying anything to them?" He replied, "Well, you can't hold people accountable for everything."

> Here's my opinion: If you're not going to hold people accountable for the standard, then get rid of the standard. (Maybe the say-hi-in-the-hallway rule just isn't working for you.) It's better not to have a standard in place than to have it and not hold people accountable for it; it looks insincere and makes employees think other standards can be ignored, too.

Remember, when times are challenging, standards are more critical than ever. When times are tough, old behaviors can creep back in. Standards help you "keep it together" in the face of adversity and present a calm, professional, united front to the world. That's why good leaders take their Standards of Behavior seriously—and make sure others do too.

CHAPTER ELEVEN TOOL:

EMPLOYEE FORUMS

When NASA is preparing to send up a space shuttle, they spend plenty of time making sure the craft is set to go and everybody is aligned. Before they blast that shuttle into space, they make sure everyone involved truly understands the external environment. The same principle holds when a plane takes off. The pilot makes sure that everything is aligned internally and carefully checks the external weather pattern. Air traffic controllers are also aligned.

These same issues—alignment and the external environment—are just as critical to healthcare organizations striving to improve performance. Regular employee forums allow us to address both.

It's important to build an "external environment" component into every employee forum you hold. Discuss the improvements that are being made in your organization and the challenges you face based on changes that are happening in the external environment.

Such forums collectively make up one of the keys to true transparency, a concept that excellent organizations role model.

Why Transparency Matters

We find that while many C-Suite leaders know just how bad the external environment has gotten and what it means for their organization, others may not grasp the implications as fully.

That's a major disconnect. When managers and staff don't have a solid grasp of the larger context in which they're working, how can we expect them to function as true partners with C-Suite leaders?

In order to align resources and move with the right amount of urgency, the entire organization needs to have the same view of the external environment. We must strive for transparency in decision making.

Employees, too, need to know what's going on in the external environment. If they don't know, they assume the worst and certainly hear and read the worst from the media. Or they may assume the environment won't impact their organization or their unit. That means they won't be on top of their game. They'll be disengaged. They won't execute their goals or provide the extraordinary patient care needed in a tough economy. Overwhelmed by fear or overconfidence, they simply *can't* or won't.

Employee forums allow the C-Suite to directly inform and educate staff at all levels on the external environment. Knowing what's happening, and what it means, is always better than not knowing. Plus, telling employees the facts kicks the organization out of "Park Ranger Leadership" mode and motivates everyone to take ownership of their own destiny.

Forums Are Great Learning Opportunities.

In general, forums help employees and volunteers understand the financial impact of what is going on outside and inside their organization. Leaders have the opportunity to explain how the budget is created, how pay raises are determined, how new equipment decisions are made, and so forth. Leaders can also explain that the organization as a whole will have to perform better in order to handle the pay raises and purchase the new equipment.

When I was president of Baptist Hospital, I found forums to be really gratifying. In less than one year, we turned an employee group that had very little understanding of the organization finances into near experts.

After these forums, they knew the bond ratings, the interest rates paid on our bonds, cash flow needs, money collection goal, and that cash needed to be collected on a daily basis in order to cover cost. They also knew how many days' cash on hand we had, in terms of both amount and number of days.

We even discussed the cash on hand goal and we connected it back to them and how much cash on hand they would want for their family. Making this analogy really helped them connect the dots on why knowing these financial elements is so important. And in the end, for any healthcare organization, being a good financial steward is key to providing excellent patient care and excellent overall operations.

Don't Assume They Already Know the External Environment.

> Most employees will be very surprised at what they hear in forums. In fact, organizations always hear a couple of "ah-has" when staff see that the revenue collected is so much less than what is charged. As a senior leader you might think, *Oh, gee, everybody knows that.* But that just is not the case.

Senior executives are so close to the finances and the pressures caused by the external environment that it is easy to assume others are seeing and feeling the same way. And one of those assumptions has to do with the perceptions of employees. Very rarely do people truly understand the difference between what their organization collects and what it charges. They usually think the organization is making more money than it actually is.

Another point of confusion for employees is money is tight, but then they see a brand new building going up or a new parking lot being put in. Or they see the press releases and press conferences that mention the $30 million building going up or a new $1.5 million piece of equipment being purchased.

Employees get confused because they hear that things are really rough for the organization, yet they see money being spent. This just wouldn't happen in their own lives. After all, when money is tight in their family budget, they don't even think about adding a room to their house, expanding the driveway, or buying a brand new car.

Of course, healthcare organizations make these decisions to expand their mission or to put in new practices and procedures that will generate revenue for the organization. A building is renovated because it will help the organization be more cost efficient. IT software is purchased because it will increase efficiency and reduce labor costs. Essentially, the organization spends money to make money, a concept that can be difficult for some employees to grasp.

In the context of their own lives, employees typically don't think about spending money to make money. Unlike a workplace, a family is probably not going to lay anyone off. And it's not that employees don't know this, it's that they haven't thought about the matter in quite that way. By connecting the dots for staff, leaders can stave off resentment and prevent we/they divisiveness.

Forums Help Us "Connect the Dots" for Staff.

A hospital had a mother/baby maternity unit that was in desperate need of remodeling. Unfortunately, the neighborhood where the hospital was located did not have the best payer mix. At the same time, a decision was made to build a brand new outpatient facility several miles from the main campus in a neighborhood with a better payer mix. (You can see where this is going!)

Administration decided to meet with the mother/baby unit staff to discuss that money was just too tight to provide the renovations. And they knew they would also need to explain why they were going out and spending $20 million-plus on an outpatient facility miles from their hospital. Yes, it promised to be a tough sell!

A well-planned meeting ended up saving them. They met with all of the acute care facility employees and explained why the outpatient facility was being built. During this forum they showed staff that because of the payer mix in the hospital's area they did not have the cash flow to finance internal renovations. However, by building the new facility in an area with a better payer mix where they could be more profitable, they would eventually be able to increase the cash flow and renovate the inside of *their* hospital.

In less than three years the mother/baby unit was completely remodeled based on the success of the outpatient pavilion. Had they not been able to explain the financial situation to the acute care employees, they would have been upset that the people in the outpatient pavilion were getting all of the resources. The forum headed that problem off at the pass.

By explaining the external environment, sharing what was being done to meet its financial challenges, discussing the plan's advantages, and giving them some "what's in it for me" perspective, they gained the support of the hospital employees. They hoped that the outpatient facility would be successful and told all their friends and neighbors to utilize it. This situation was a real win/win for the organization.

Share Your Challenges... and Enlist Support.

Here's another example of how powerful employee forums can be. This story centers on a hospital in a three-hospital town. A national insurance company that covered the hospital plus one other in town announced one day that it was going to start covering the third hospital.

Basically, the market would be divided up by thirds instead of in half, which obviously would mean a decrease in paying patients. Also, there would be a 20 percent reduction in reimbursement. Oh, and the insurance company was making it optional. The hospital could stay with the plan, which was the market leader, or the insurance provider would take the patients elsewhere. Essentially, it could take less or none at all.

Administration met with the employees and told them what was happening and what it meant for the organization. They explained what the hospital was going to have to do, and started harvesting ideas from staff on cost savings, revenue enhancements, and so forth. The employees were clear on why the decision was made. By explaining all aspects to staff, the hospital gained staff support and made them a part of finding solutions.

So how did it all turn out? Well, obviously the insurance change brought about some new challenges. But the hospital staff responded well and, in the end, the impact was less than originally anticipated.

Do an "External Environment (EE) Check" with Managers and Staff.

Of course, keeping employees apprised on the external environment is the responsibility not just of senior leaders but all managers throughout an organization's hierarchy. C-Suite leaders can use employee forums as a means for making sure department directors and managers are cascading information properly.

At employee forums always ask your employees whether their leaders have shared recent financial news with them and connected it to the external environment. (I think of this as the "EE Check.")

Ask them: "Did they tell you what reimbursement was going to be happening? What the pay raise is going to look like and the impact it will have?" Or if the bonds have been upgraded or downgraded: "Did they tell you what the bond rate increase or decrease will mean to the organization?"

Forums Are for Celebrating, Too!

One day we received great news. The hospital bond rating had gone up. That meant that we could let staff know that $1.6 million would be added to our bottom line because they had done such a great job managing operations. Naturally, adding that money to the bottom line would help the hospital be an even better organization.

Employee forums aren't just about sharing bad news. They're about celebrating great news, too. Either way, employee forums are absolutely necessary.

We recommend that C-suite leaders bring their employee groups together every 90 days to explain to them what's going on with the organization's external environment. (Thanks to technology like video streaming, virtual employees and others who miss the actual meetings don't have to miss the important messages shared.)

> The more employees understand, the healthier the culture, the better the performance, and the better the outcomes will be. It's that simple—and that powerful.

Sample Employee Forum Agenda

I. Welcome and Staff Recognition	
II. External Environment Update:	Improvements Challenges Next Steps
III. Pillar / Outcome Update:	Service: • Patient Perception of Care Results • Physician Satisfaction Results Quality: • Ventilator Pneumonia • Hospital-Acquired Infections • Falls Finance: • Productivity • Operating Income People: • Turnover • Employee Satisfaction Update • Benefit Update Growth: • Market Share Community: • Philanthropy
IV. Closing and Final Recognition	

StuderGroup

Figure 11.1: Sample Employee Forum Agenda

CHAPTER TWELVE TOOL:

COMMUNICATION BOARDS

T hroughout this book praises have been sung about the need for creating transparent organizations. Transparency is important even in the best of times. Frank Sacco, the CEO of Memorial Healthcare System in Hollywood, Florida, says this. I asked Frank the keys to his organization's success. They have lots. His first response: "Transparency." He added, "Transparency creates accountability."

In the face of a challenging external environment, transparency is even more important. All employees need to know what's going on with their organization at any given moment.

> Think about it. Employees who know revenue is down and patient satisfaction results are falling are more likely to do their best work. They see the urgency and respond to it. That's why, for all their simplicity, communication boards are such valuable tools. They create

more transparent organizations. Every unit
should have one.

I'm talking about actual "bulletin board" type areas
in which up-to-date information is posted. (Someone
once asked me why I promote physical rather than virtual
boards. It's not that I have anything against the Internet.
I don't. In fact, it may be a great idea to post the same information on your internal website. I simply believe that
healthcare is a physical, hands-on field, so naturally the
people who work in it like to have a place to go and stand
and look at tangible hard copy, photos, and graphics.)

Employees Like Communication Boards.

Years ago I worked at a hospital that really made a big
deal out of communication boards. We asked every manager to keep his or her board updated with monthly and
year-to-date financial reports. We found that employees
really appreciated having access to these numbers. It was
like having a "snapshot" of the organization's bottom
line.

One employee in facilities told me he really liked seeing the hospital's financial information. In fact, he had
gotten so good at reading it that he used it to plan his
own finances. He knew that if we had a month when we
didn't hit budget or if our year-to-date figures were not
looking good, he wouldn't get any overtime for a while.
This allowed his family to plan accordingly.

On the other hand, I've also had people say, "Well,
you know, Quint, I don't know if these communication

boards are working because I'm not sure everybody is looking at them."

> No, you can't be sure everybody reads your organization's communication boards, but you *can* be sure they know the information and data are there. Some people *will* read it. If nothing else, the process of keeping the boards updated will ensure that managers are constantly aware of what's going on in your organization and that the external environment stays "top of mind."

Setting up Your Boards

As I mentioned, every department should have its own communication board that's kept up to date. It should include information on the external environment, changes that are being made in order to respond to it, relevant articles, and updates on how well the organization is doing with patient care.

If your organization uses the Five Pillars of Excellence model for goal-setting, you might consider having your boards reflect that structure. In other words, every board would be divided into the following sections: Finance, Quality, People, Growth, and Service. Some organizations like to add a sixth Community section as well.

Be sure to give the external environment its own place of honor on the boards. Some leaders prefer to place a standalone External Environment section at the top, which visually demonstrates that all internal decisions are connected to the bigger picture. Others prefer to create external environment sub-sections under each pillar. Do whatever works best for you.

What to include under each pillar:

EXTERNAL ENVIRONMENT: Post articles on changes in financial payments, technology, trends, and so forth.

SERVICE: Here you might post scores and information relating to satisfaction levels of various groups: patients, physicians, and other departments your department serves.

QUALITY: List quality indicators for each department, the goal for each indicator, and the current status of each indicator.

FINANCE: Include information about how the individual department is doing as well as how the entire organization is doing. As mentioned earlier, this provides everyone with a useful snapshot of the financial bottom line.

PEOPLE: Post information about new hires, turnover, and overtime. Include ideas to help employees see the impact they, the people in the trenches, have in the department.

<u>GROWTH</u>: Include information on the number of patients being seen and where improvements are needed. You might offer suggestions on how to reduce the number of people who leave your ED without being seen or how to reduce the number of no-shows in your outpatient units.

<u>COMMUNITY</u>: Include articles that show the impact the organization has in the local community, philanthropically and in other ways. This is also a great place to post information about the external environment!

Keeping Boards Current

When you change the information regularly, employees will start to really pay attention to communication boards so as not to miss anything interesting or important. As I alluded to earlier, I think department managers should be in charge of keeping their boards updated, because it keeps them on top of the organization's status.

At one time I worked with a surgical leader named Brenda Traywick. She really knew how to manage a communication board. Not only was it always up to date, she knew exactly how to get the employees' attention. She prioritized the information on the board. If something was important she marked it in yellow. Naturally, her employees' eyes were drawn to the highlighted information first.

If it was doubly important, she had it underlined in yellow and starred with an asterisk. If it was triple important, she had both these markings plus a little arrow pointing to something she had written like, "Great job!" or "Look at our OR turnaround. We've got it under 15 minutes!"

In other words, Brenda took her communication board from being just a bunch of information to being a valuable tool that showed me, an employee, exactly what I should look at and what I should prioritize. If you follow her lead, you won't regret it.

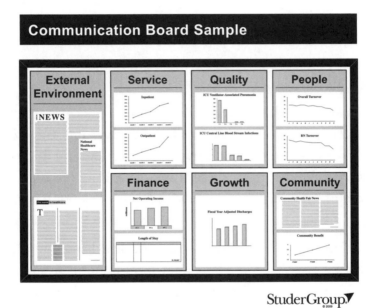

Figure 12.1 Communication Boards

CHAPTER THIRTEEN TOOL:

NEWSLETTERS

I like newsletters. They are good communication tactics. However, in all my years in the healthcare industry, I've rarely seen one used to its full potential so that it will impact people's behavior.

You may have noticed this about your own newsletter. Whenever an employee attitude survey shows poor scores in the communication category, often others will point to the marketing department or PR person and complain that the newsletter isn't doing its job!

I believe newsletters (printed or online) can be *extremely* valuable tools for conveying information about the external environment to your employees. They just need to be used more effectively.

Too many organizations use their newsletters as "data downloads" and photo ops for senior leaders. They may print a few facts about the external environment, but they fail to connect the dots for employees, physicians, and volunteers. Even if they explain what the organization is doing to respond to external changes, they may not tell the reader what he or she should do individually.

Four Tips for Creating Newsletters That Work

The good news is it's not that difficult to change the way your newsletter is used. Here are a few pointers:

1) *Include important articles.* In each newsletter, prominently place an article about the industry and the organization's external environment. Those types of stories update your employees and your physicians on the context they're working in.

2) *Write about things that can be done to react to the external environment.* I have a newspaper with a headline that reads, "Broad Brush Hurricane Ivan Steers Towards Pensacola." In fact, I know that I had a copy of that newspaper on my dining room table when my family and I evacuated because when we came back to look at our house after the hurricane, there it was sitting on the table. See! The newspaper told me what was happening with my external environment. And, of course, it also told me exactly what I should do to minimize damage and ensure my own safety and that of my family.

In your newsletter, provide steps for how employees should react to changes in the external environment. Include success stories from inside the organization. Share the good decisions people are already making so that they can serve as role models to everyone else. Providing examples of people inside your organization who are ad justing and making changes sends the message that readers can do the same.

> Make it clear that employees shouldn't assume that "somebody else" is solving the organization's problems. There are very intelligent people in every organization who show up every day and adjust to what is going on. When staff understand the external environment and feel empowered to respond to it with positive action—and get recognized for doing so—more action is sure to follow.

3) *Provide links to other articles about the external environment.* The quicker people get excited about learning about the external environment, the quicker the organization will get aligned and the better reactions it will have.

4) *Don't assume that leaders are using the newsletter in staff conversations.* Send a note out prior to the newsletter's release. Tell your leaders that the newsletter is coming out, walk them through the key articles they should be aware of, and then very specifically ask them to carry the newsletter with them when they are talking and rounding with staff.

Teach them when they round to pull the newsletter out, show the key articles, and ask, "Have you read this?" "What are your thoughts?" "Ideas?"

The same thing applies if the newsletter is available online. Have them ask their employees if they pulled it up and read it. In other words, leaders should know that their goal is not just to make sure that the newsletter has been distributed; it's to make sure that the employees have read and absorbed it.

More Ways to Use Newsletters

Leaders can also make time to discuss newsletter articles at their department meetings. It's important that they focus not on the newsletter as a whole but on specific articles. Again, it's all about connecting dots, engaging staff, and harvesting and answering tough questions.

Make sure the newsletter goes up on the department communication board under the heading "External Environment." If your communication board is structured around the pillars, you may want to put the "External Environment" section up above the pillars. After all, the external environment is going to impact all of the pillars and all organization actions.

> You may have many other ideas. The point is to make the newsletter more than the house organ. Instead, make it a living leadership tool and technique that can be used to help people understand the external environment, react properly to changes that occur, and align resources in order to achieve desired results.

SECTION THREE:

SENIOR LEADER TOOLKIT

A ll leaders have important roles to play. Senior leaders, however, set the tone for the rest of the organization. If they are not aligned and in sync, no one else can be.

This section provides a series of exercises to help senior leaders diagnose their own performance, better understand how change impacts the organization, and explore ways to become even more effective.

Exercises included in Section 3 are:
- Formulating the Organizational Grade Point
- Creative Tension
- What's in It for Me?
- Always, Usually, Sometimes, and Never
- What Does Being On Board Look Like?

These exercises will help senior leaders stay grounded, objective, and mentally agile—all qualities needed to guide the organization to success in a shifting external environment.

CHAPTER FOURTEEN:

SENIOR LEADER TOOLKIT

O ver the years we have been fortunate to work with many organizations. More often than not, they are already pretty good, with most being well known for out-standing results in many areas. So what do already good organizations have in common? They are not content with their results, even if those results are outstanding. They always are searching to get better.

These organizations are led by individuals who want results, but who also want to put in place a framework and systems to enable excellent results to be sustained long after they leave the organization.

Jim Collins' book *Built to Last* is a good way to describe these leaders. They want the organizational culture to be one that adapts to the environment while holding on to its core values.

While many organizations are recognized publicly for their results, there is no doubt that many factors impact results—locations, payer mix, and past history to name a few. While top 100 lists are nice, if too much attention is placed on one component, many deserving organizations may not appear on the list. Of course, to most organizations making a list is not the be-all end-all. Most leaders focus not on awards but on making sure the organization meets its mission: to be the best organization it can become.

So what characteristics are most common in those organizations that achieve excellent results across the board? While observation is good, observation combined with data is better.

In 2004, the Alliance for Healthcare Research (now named the Studer Alliance for Healthcare Research) studied high-performing organizations. The criteria were that the organizations must have excellent results in service, quality, people, finance, and growth and must have maintained them for at least three years.

The study found that the top five factors that impacted performance were as follows:

One, senior leadership displayed a commitment to excellence. High-performing organizations were all led by people who were relentless in achieving outcomes. As I wrote in a recent blog, they would adapt behavior to achieve the goal, not lower the goal to meet the behavior.

The second attribute was that every organization had in place an objective leader evaluation system.

Third was an investment in leadership skill development.

Fourth, these companies had robust systems of transparent staff communication, including consistent methods to provide information and gain input from staff.

The fifth item listed was a conscious effort to connect the dots to the why. These organizations did not assume it is evident to the staff that what they do has great impact. They had techniques in place via stories, videos, and so forth to connect the staff to the impact they and the organization had on people's lives.

There were other items listed but these are the top five.

Periodically people will come up to me and ask, "Isn't change better if it comes from the bottom, from a grassroots effort?" My reply is, "Yes, if senior leaders allow it to happen."

No doubt the key is to have all staff in an organization, or at least the great majority of staff at all levels and roles, committed to achieving the organization's goals and adapting to the changes needed to achieve them. However, the senior leader, and most significantly the CEO, is in charge of components necessary to achieve such results.

The CEO sets the agenda. While the board of any organization is vital, the day-to-day person who sets the organization agenda is the CEO, followed by the leaders of each area.

Second, there will be no change in the leader evaluation system (which also impacts the CEO), without the CEO's approval. We have even found that some members of the C-Suite will push back on an objective evaluation system. There is an inherent fear of how they will do. This change is usually driven by the CEO.

Third, the investment in leader development needs to be approved and driven by the CEO.

An organization can have components of excellence and periods of excellence, but without senior leaders' actions, it will not have consistent and lasting excellence.

With this knowledge it became evident that organizations would benefit from a senior leader toolkit. Such a kit would help the senior leadership team get aligned in their understanding of current performance and in the actions needed to best achieve and maintain consistent excellence.

This is why we've created a number of tactics that can be used by all leaders. You've already seen a few of these, and now we will provide more senior leader-focused exercises.

Exercise: Formulating the Organizational Grade Point

There are a number of exercises that help leadership teams gain a greater understanding of themselves and what it will take to create excellence in an organization. It's certain that the external environment will keep changing, and that definitely affects the ability to lead an organization.

It's not usual to hear the CEO introduce the senior leadership by saying what a great team they have. It can be heard that the organization is excellent. It can be heard so often it may affect objectivity.

Knox Singleton, the long-term CEO of Inova Health System in Virginia and someone I respect greatly, once said, "CEOs have to be very careful that after awhile you don't become a legend in your own mind by over-evaluating your own performance."

To me, a truly "great team" consistently puts in a winning performance. Great students get great grades, so let's grade the organization's results objectively. And that's why I like this exercise, called the Pillar Grade Point Average. It lets us all see whether the praise a team is hearing is justified, or whether it's more hype.

First, post the Pillars of Excellence in the meeting room where everyone can easily see them. (You can use a flip chart if you wish; personally, I think it's more fun.) If the pillars are not used, then use whatever objective organizational goals are in place. We use Service, Quality, Finance, People, and Growth.

Then you go around the room and have each person provide a grade for each goal. It will lead to some discussion, for often people in the room will not agree. It is good for the top-ranking leader in the room to go last; if not, I find that the group is swayed by the grade this leader gives.

For example, when I was working with one organization—one where the participants were introduced as "a great leadership team" prior to starting this exercise—I asked, "How would you evaluate service, using patient satisfaction as the example?" Well, since they had just brought us in to help them, it wasn't surprising that they gave themselves a grade between a C and a D. We ended up agreeing on a C.

Next, we went around the room and talked about the Quality pillar. They gave themselves a B. This was no surprise either, as I've never been in any healthcare organization that ranks their quality below a B!

When we got to Finance, they gave themselves a strong B.

Then we talked about the People pillar, specifically employee satisfaction and turnover, and they gave themselves a C.

Finally, we talked about Growth. This organization had done an exceptional job in this area by attracting specialists in their large city to shift patients to them. Therefore, they gave themselves an A. This also helped gain the increased financial results.

To sum up, they gave themselves two Cs, which together equal 4 points, two Bs, which equal 6 points, and one A, which is 4 points. The total is 14. So we divided 14 by 5 and got 2.8.

So basically, this team gave itself a 2.8 grade point average.

Service	Quality	Finance	People	Growth
C	B	B	C	A
2	3	3	2	4

$$2 + 3 + 3 + 2 + 4 = 14 \text{ pts}$$
$$14\text{pts} / 5 = 2.8 \text{ GPA}$$

Then I asked the team if they thought a 2.8 grade point average signified great performance. They all agreed that no, it did not. This led to a very good discussion about how we tend to think if we do really well on one pillar, we can say we're great across the board. We all agreed this did not make logical sense.

I find organizations tend to use the term "great" when they're describing financial performance and not necessarily performance across the system. Generally, if we're great in the service realm but not doing so well financially, we don't say we're a great organization.

This exercise is meant to allow a senior executive team to see themselves as they really are, not as they want to be introduced. In fact, every time I see the executive I worked with on this particular exercise, he says, "Quint, I'll never call ourselves a great team again until we truly *are* a great team."

More importantly, he is led to have a specific discussion on actions to move all the results toward "A" performance.

That's what this exercise does. It helps hold up the mirror to current performance and leads to specific actions to move the organizational performance forward.

Exercise: Creative Tension

This exercise is aimed at showing what happens when an organization is striving to improve its level of performance. I've taken this concept from Peter Senge, who talks about creative tension in his book *The Fifth Discipline*.

Those who find the phrase "creative tension" not to their liking can use the word "disequilibrium." A main job of any leader is to manage the disequilibrium or tension in the organization. In fact, I believe it is a main job to create it in order to improve results. Staying the same will not lead to improvement. Even when an organization is "already there," there will always be pressure to stay ahead of the curve.

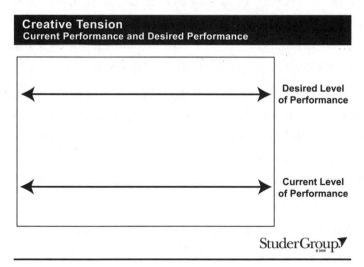

Figure 14.1: Creative Tension – Current Performance and Desired Performance

In looking at Figure 14.1, there are two parallel lines with an empty space between them. The bottom line represents the organization's average current performance. The top line represents where the organization wants the outcomes to be.

Place dots to represent where your leaders currently fall on the spectrum. Some leaders will probably fall below the current performance (CP) line. Most will be right on or near the current performance line (remember, it represents the average of all leader performance). Some leaders will be above the CP line—in fact, a few may be considerably above the line.

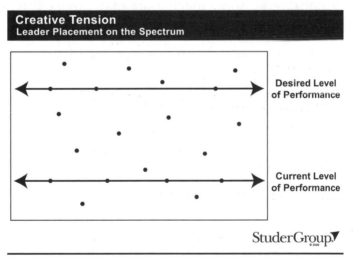

Figure 14.2: Creative Tension – Leader Placement on the Spectrum

If an organization's performance doesn't constantly get better, the changing external environment will cause it to get worse. Remember the analogy of standing still on a downward moving escalator? So organizations must constantly move toward their desired performance (DP).

The point of this exercise is to show that when we frame leadership performance in terms of moving toward the DP line, there will be anxiety in the organization. Why? Because it becomes very clear that outside of the already high performers, the vast majority of people are not meeting the new desired performance. Previously, you probably saw it as only a few people not meeting current performance...but now the bar has been raised.

So when the bar is raised, it creates anxiety. It is evident the majority of individuals will need to make changes to some degree, some much more than others. But how much anxiety can people stand?

Peter Senge says senior teams want to raise the bar to the level that it is evident that staying the same is not an option, yet not so much as to paralyze people. If we stick with the status quo, we'll automatically lower the bar to the point that we don't achieve our desired goals. High-performing organizations move their behavior to reach the goal. Others move the goal to meet the behavior.

The following graphic shows how people move.

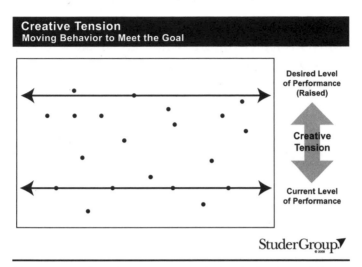

Figure 14.3: Creative Tension – Moving Behavior to Meet the Goal

Your high-performing leaders will move toward desired performance more quickly than everyone else. Some are already there. They have more skill and more self-confidence and need less of a change to get there. Others will stay where they are. And here's where organizations often make a mistake. Instead of working to move their middle performers to the new, higher level, they get hung up on focusing the majority of their time on the lower performers.

When working with an organization, our coaches attempt to spend most of the time with those people in the middle performer area. If an organization moves the middle performers up, it has taken care of the bulk of the people, and that's when the tension gets lower. Middle performers are also more likely to be coachable and to appreciate the development.

Attempting to move the skill or will of only the low performers will take quite a while. And if the middle performers are not moving up, too much of the critical mass is too far away from the desired goal, and this wears down the organization.

What Happens During Creative Tension?

- Increase in anxiety
- People who thought they had made enough changes realize they need to improve more
- Natural desire by many to lower the bar
- Feeling of "too much on plate"

StuderGroup▼

Figure 14.4: What Happens During Creative Tension?

If you don't move the middle performers up, and if you don't then move the low performers up in performance or out, the organization will suffer. Senge's research shows it takes only a small group of low performers to pull down a majority of middle and high performers. Eventually those people will get tired of striving to improve.

How does creative tension manifest? You'll most likely hear such statements as, "I have too much on my plate," "Everybody is overwhelmed," "Some are getting it and some are not." You want to listen to that feedback and provide training. Be very careful, though. Remember that the goal of the low performers is to have you lower your desired goals in order to eliminate or at least reduce creative tension.

Low performers win if the organization stays the same. The patients, families, other staff and physicians, volunteers, and the community lose.

Creative Tension - Treatment Plan

- Try to drive as few behaviors as possible for the greatest change
- Might not be "more things" but continue to improve execution (repetition creates excellence)
- Very specific development
- Continued communication back to the "why"

StuderGroup▼

Figure 14.5: Creative Tension – Treatment Plan

Exercise: What's in It for Me?

Thomas Mayer, an Emergency Department physician and a Studer Group medical adviser, said to me, "Quint, when I work in the ED, if staff and physicians see that changes will make their job easier—that there's something in it for them—they are more likely to change their behavior."

The "What's in it for me?" principle is what inspired this next exercise.

Exercise: What is in it for me?

What does this mean to:

Leaders:	
Employees:	
Physicians:	
Patients and families:	
Board Members:	
Community:	

StuderGroup▼

Figure 14.6: What's in It for Me?

People in healthcare don't necessarily like to talk about what's in it for us. We generally are not comfortable with what could appear to be self-centered thinking. But because we're all human, people do think, *How will this affect me?* Therefore, helping people see the personal impact of what is being asked leads to quicker, more enthusiastic implementation of any change.

When I was talking with some nurses, they mentioned their organization was introducing hourly rounding on patients to the staff. As the discussion went on, I brought up some information they did not appear to be aware of. I shared that a September 2006 article in the *American Journal of Nursing* reported a study on hourly rounding that showed when organizations put the tactic in place, call lights went down over 37 percent, the average nurse walked 1.4 less miles per shift, patient falls decreased 50 percent, and hospital-acquired decubiti went down 14 percent. So while the adjustment is not easy, once rounding is in place, there are some real benefits for the patients and the staff.

The nurses quickly said they had not been familiar with this data, but now that they were they could see why hourly rounding was being put in place. The job of leaders is to help people understand not just the *what* and the *how* but also the *why*—and what impact the change will have on them, their patients, and the organization as a whole. The more the value of a new tool, technique, and/or process can be shown, the better the execution of the change will be.

Helping people discover the "what's in it for each group" is time well spent and is valuable beyond the C-Suite. For the C-Suite it is vital, for it gets the team aligned to the actions, the benefits, and the key message points. Depending on size, the group can go through each entity together or break into smaller groups with each group taking an entity and then reporting out.

What's in It for Leaders?

First of all, when implementing Evidence-Based Leadership practices, what's in it for a leader? Answers might include: a better objective measurement tool (accountability, which in the organizational assessment this book is based on, always ranks in the top two of opportunities to improve) and the fact that the objective goals, evaluation system, and standards identify the priorities. Leaders also find that the training helps them be better performers, which then reduces anxiety. These things all lead to consistency, which creates excellence.

The leader will also enjoy better interdepartmental working relationships. Systems will work better. People will have the tools and equipment to do the job or they understand why they are not there. Low performance is addressed, which makes life easier for everyone. Ultimately, the organization achieves its goals, which means there are more resources and things continue to get better.

What Does This Mean to Leaders?

- Specific outcomes are in place (reduces distractions)
- Priorities are understood
- Increased skills for success (better use of time)
- Better inter-department workings (efficiency)
- Better tools and equipment to do the job (effectiveness)
- Better feeling about being a lead

Equals:
- Better leader satisfaction
- Better operational performance across the board

StuderGroup▼

Figure 14.7: What Does This Mean to Leaders?

What's in It for Employees?

The number one thing employees want is a good leader. If they have a good leader, systems work, tools and equipment are provided so they can do their job, they get rewarded and recognized, and receive professional development. Also, departments are working well together, they are getting thank-you notes, reward and recognition, and they are not held back by leaders and staff with performance issues.

What Does This Mean to Employees?

- Better relationship with leader and more confidence in administration
- Understand how the organization is operating
- Understand actions needed to improve/sustain the gain
- Feel better about where they work
- Systems work better
- Tools and equipment to do the job
- More reward and recognition
- More effective and efficient because decreased new people

Equals:
- Decreased turnover
- Decreased use of overtime
- Decreased absenteeism
- Increased operational performance across the board
- Better work/life balance
- Better handoffs and explanation

StuderGroup▼

Figure 14.8: What Does It Mean to Employees?

What's in It for Physicians?

If you've read my book *Hardwiring Excellence* and Dr. Stephen Beeson's books, *Practicing Excellence* and *Engaging Physicians*—it is evident that there is quite a bit. Physicians have a lot to gain from organizational excellence. It is not uncommon after initial skepticism for physicians to say, "I have been telling them (administration) that for years." When physicians see the data, they very quickly see the positive impact of organizations' implementing Evidence-Based Leadership and Practices.

Physicians want: quality care for the patients, efficient, effective places to practice medicine, input into decisions, and at least some acknowledgment and recognition for their work.

Hearing the benefits of the tools and techniques to improve execution, thus organizational performance, is music to their ears. One win is a reduction in patient no-shows due to the pre-visit phone calls. Another is a decrease in non-reimbursed patient re-admissions due to post-visit phone calls.

Data shows that when physicians are rounded on by leaders to make sure they have what is needed to provide patient care, they feel better about practicing medicine and are more likely to recommend the organization to patients and to colleagues. It is about execution.

Best of all, they experience a more reliable organization. No longer is there a day hospital, a night hospital, a weekend hospital, a holiday hospital...or a day clinic and night clinic...or a nursing home or residential facility that runs smoothly one day but not the next. That consistency makes life easier for them and also for their patients.

Because there is a preference card for all physicians, not just surgeons, the practice environment is more conducive to excellent patient care.

You see, there's quite a bit in it for physicians!

What Does This Mean to Physicians?

- Reduced patient no-shows
- Decreased non-reimbursed patient re-admissions
- Physicians have what they need to take care of patients
- Patients are more satisfied with care
- Decreased complications, litigation, and time
- Greater peace of mind
- Increased consistency and a more effective and efficient place to practice medicine

Equals:
- Better performance financially
- Better fulfillment of physician mission to provide better care for patient
- Better clinical quality

StuderGroup

Figure 14.9: What Does This Mean to Physicians?

What's in It for Patients?

The answer is simple: Patients are getting a better place to receive care.

What Does This Mean to Patients?

- A better place to receive care
- Anxiety is reduced
- Pain is being managed
- Call lights are being responded to
- Medications are understood
- Improved communication with families
- Understand their home care instructions

Equals:

- Meeting mission and vision with the organization and as person
- Fewer re-admissions
- Increased market share

StuderGroup▼

Figure 14.10: What Does This Mean to Patients?

Implement AIDET and other key words, and patients benefit the following ways.

A: They are **Acknowledged** by name, which leads to better safety and helps them feel more cared about.

I: Hearing each person's skill set and experience when care providers **Introduce** themselves decreases the patient's anxiety, which leads to improved listening and compliance. When it's time to see a physician, a staff member introduces him or her by saying something like, "This is a doctor I'd want my father to go to." (Fortunately, 99 percent of the time people in healthcare feel very good about managing up others!)

D: The patients and their families hear how long things will take **(Duration)**—how long it will be before they are seen, how long it will take, how long it will be before they can leave, when they will learn the results.

E: Patients have each item **Explained** in a way that is understandable and questions are answered. They are told what's being done, why it's being done, how it's being done, and by whom it is being done.

T: The patients are **Thanked** for choosing that organization or for being helpful, understanding, and so forth.

But the benefits of AIDET are only the beginning of what's in it for the patient. Leaders will round on them every day to make sure the care is excellent or to find out what can be improved. Positive comments on staff and physicians will be heard and then relayed to these individuals, which reinforces the excellence. The patient may also be rounded on by staff hourly, which means the likelihood of falling is greatly reduced.

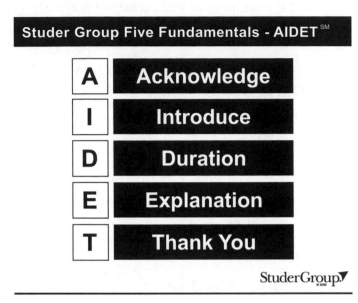

Figure 14.11: Studer Group Five Fundamentals - AIDET[SM]

Patients may get a pre-visit phone call to make sure they have the right time and location and know what to bring so the visit can be productive. In the doctor's office they may even fill out a patient visit agenda guide, which will make for a much better visit. Dr. Beeson's book *Practicing Excellence* offers an example of this.

Depending on the situation, a patient may receive a post-care phone call to make sure everything is understood, from the medication prescribed to the details surrounding the next visit.

What's in It for Board Members?

The number one thing a board wants to do is fulfill its fiduciary responsibility by overseeing a good, solid, profitable organization. A key part of doing this is making sure systems are in place to evaluate performance. Board members want to take comfort that patients are receiving excellent care, resources are being used correctly, physicians have confidence in the organization, and the organization is meeting and/or exceeding all local, state, and federal guidelines. It is also nice to hear that the staff feels they work for a good organization.

So what else is in it for board members? They have the reassurance of knowing that leaders are being well trained.

They get to walk around the community and not hear horror stories about the ED; instead, they hear positive comments about it.

They get to feel very good knowing their success isn't built solely on the CEO they currently have. It's built on putting a system in place that will be sustainable not only after every executive leaves but also after board members leave. Its success is built not on personalities, but on performance. The best succession plan in the world is when all leaders in an organization have the skill via training and mentoring to be successful.

What Does This Mean to Board Members?

- A clear way to better evaluate the CEO
- Balanced approach to performance with key metrics
- Improved patient care
- Improved financial stewardship
- Improved relationship with physicians

Equals:

- Better clinical outcomes for patients
- Increased operational performance
- Increased market share
- Increased philanthropy and giving

StuderGroup

Figure 14.12: What Does This Mean to Board Members?

This exercise helps you spell it out to each group so that they'll get on board and throw all of their passion and commitment into the change effort. For board members it also creates that commitment to have strong legs, knowing that improving performance will require dedication, strong determination, and the understanding that there will be bumps along the way.

What's in It for the Community?

Every community with a healthcare organization wants to be able to count on the fact that services provided are excellent and offered at a competitive price. Each community wants the provider to operate well, for not only does it provide a vital service to the community, it is also a major employer. Great healthcare organizations equal a healthier community, in more ways than one.

Communities take great pride when the healthcare organization in their area is known for excellence. It's comforting to know that, if needed, help is there. A well-run organization creates jobs and attracts businesses and families. We have all heard stories of people living in a certain place in order to have access to excellent healthcare.

In her book, *Excellence in the Emergency Department*, author Stephanie Baker describes how her family moved in order for her to be healthier. In quality of life studies, access to healthcare is a key attribute, an important part of people's perception that their community has a good quality of life.

So if a community were to ask, "What's in it for me?" some answers would be: Access to high-quality care at a competitive cost; a solid area employer, a must-have in terms of economic development, and a contributor to many community organizations. That's a lot!

What Does This Mean to the Community?

- Better access to care for patients
- Better place to work for employees
- Healthier community
- Better place for physicians to practice medicine

Equals:

- High-quality care at a competitive cost
- A community that has a positive workforce at a major employer (healthcare)

StuderGroup▼

Figure 14.13: What Does It Mean to the Community?

Exercise: Always, Usually, Sometimes, and Never

When there is a story about an incident in which lives are saved or damage prevented, an individual or individuals are typically highlighted for the impact they made. When US Airways Captain Chesley B. "Sully" Sullenberger safely landed the airplane he was piloting on the Hudson River, lives were saved. If not for his action, people would have died, and hundreds of families for generations to come would have been affected. Of course, this courageous result was also dependent on many others stepping up to save lives.

It seems when there is tragedy in the air it is not uncommon to read the findings as human error. One person can save lives and improve the quality of life for many. Yet it is also true that one or a few people can cause great damage. Another exercise that helps point out the need to have ALL people, particularly the senior team, on the same page is *Always, Usually, Sometimes, and Never*. Great execution is about *Always*. As with the other exercises in this chapter, this is based on the practical experience that comes from working with hundreds of organizations.

An organization we worked with early on identified employee turnover as an area that needed to be improved. In this case improvement meant lowering turnover. (You may be wondering, *Is there* ever *a time when it is good to increase turnover?* The answer is, *Yes, if performance issues have not been dealt with.*) Research shows that in most cases lower turnover leads to more efficient care as shown by decreasing lengths of stay and more effective care as demonstrated by a lower mortality index.

In the diagnostic phase, early turnover—those leaving within the first several months—was found to be too high. To decrease these early departures, the organization agreed to implement peer interviewing, behavioral-based questioning, and 30- and 90-day meetings for all new hires. As the months went on there was an overall reduction in turnover, especially in the new hires. Any CEO, and for that matter anyone from the boardroom to the hallway, would feel good about this turnover reduction. Besides the clinical advantages, it created lower overtime cost, better interdepartmental coordination, and other measurable outcomes. Still, when the numbers are moving in the right direction, it may be easy to miss areas in which the agreed upon actions are not taking place.

In this exercise, we asked the senior leader group a question to tell us how often their department did certain tactics: *Always, Usually, Sometimes,* or *Never.*

In this particular organization there are slightly over 11,000 employees, and 11 individuals sit at the senior executive table. (This symmetrical ratio is pure coincidence and does not mean that one senior leader is needed for every one thousand employees. Obviously, numbers vary by organization, depending on many factors!)

Five of the senior executives had absolutely hardwired peer interviewing. They had hardwired behavioral-based questioning, used the matrix to select new employees, and held 30- and 90-day meetings between the supervisor and each new hire. So they responded with *Always*.

(The definition of *Always* was widened to mean the above tactics took place 90 percent of the time or more, due to the actions being relatively new. For some actions *Always* would mean 100 percent right off the bat; it depended on the desired outcome, the complexity of execution, and the urgency of the situation. Eventually, *Always* would be changed to equal 100 percent.)

Four of the senior leaders said *Usually*. Now for this situation, *Usually* meant three out of every four times, or 75 percent or more. In other words most of the time potential hires were peer interviewed and they went through behavioral-based questioning. Most of the time 30- and 90-day meetings were held.

One of the leaders said *Sometimes*. *Sometimes* meant anywhere from 1 to 74 percent, and, if you're like me, what it really meant was: "Every once in a great while if I really have to or someone asks."

One leader said *Never*.

Now, at first glance, this might not seem like a bad deal. In fact, if the CEO were to look around the room and ask, "Is everybody peer interviewing and doing your 30- and 90-day meetings?" they would see five heads bobbing aggressively up and down and four heads bobbing a bit less vigorously. Most likely, upon seeing 9 out of 11 bobbing heads the thought would be, *Wow! Good job.*

(I imagine the head belonging to the *Sometimes* leader would be nodding casually and the *Never* leader might be trying to hide behind someone else, or pretending to be absorbed in some paper work and thinking, *I hope I get away with this*. So the overall effect would look pretty positive.)

If you put yourself in our hypothetical CEO's shoes, you might think 9 out 11 people *USUALLY* doing what they're supposed to be doing is pretty good. But how good is it really?

First, let's look at our leader who answered *Never*. Because of his role, 1,200 employees report to this leader in some fashion: vice presidents, department directors, his managers or supervisors, and all the people under this division in the organizational chart.

That means 1,200 out of 11,000 employees are not experiencing what the CEO is talking about at employee forums, or what they're reading about in employee newsletters, or what some of their coworkers who work in other divisions are experiencing. People often follow the example of their boss.

What about our *Sometimes* leader? This person had approximately 800 in her division. When 1,200 and 800 are added up, it equals 2,000 people. That means almost 17 to 18 percent of the employees in that organization, or almost one out of every five, were not experiencing what they were supposed to be experiencing. The results are good, but imagine how much better they could be. Also, eventually this variation in leadership will lead to a decay in performance.

Their leaders' lack of alignment was impacting them in a very real way.

Always 90-100%	Usually 75-89%	Sometimes 5-74%	Never <5%
5	4	1 ▼ 800 employees	1 ▼ 1,200 employees

Conclusion: *Total = 2,000 employees*
One in every five employees may or may not be peer interviewed.

So, if something needs to *ALWAYS* happen, make sure it is an *Always* at the senior level. And if it needs to *USUALLY* happen, make sure senior levels are answering *Usually*. If you have senior leaders who are answering *Sometimes* or *Never*, it's time to think about how much you're willing to tolerate their lack of follow-through.

It became very apparent to the CEO of a well-known Eastern healthcare system that some senior executives weren't following through. One-on-one sessions between the CEO and each direct report took place. It was explained to each direct report where the organization was headed and why. Despite its history of success, adjustments to be more consistent were necessary.

The CEO explained what they would be doing and their own commitment to the plan, and then each direct report was asked, "Are you 100 percent committed to this? Because if you're not 100 percent committed, I need to know. Then we need to talk about whether we can get you to 100 percent and what that looks like. If we can't get you to 100 percent, then we need to talk about your exiting the organization."

This directness paid off. That organization has ended up being one of the very best in the country across the board. In fact, a couple of years ago when *USA Today* wrote about great quality institutions in healthcare, this was the organization featured.

Alignment is important. If even one senior leader is not aligning his performance to the organization's expectations, and to the performance of the other senior leaders at the table, it can be very costly.

To read an Always Leadership article, please visit www.studergroup.com/StraightALeadership.

Exercise: What Does Being On Board Look Like?

I was on the West Coast at an academic medical center doing the first day of a two-day Leadership Development Institute (LDI) for an organization that has an excellent leader.

Because of the size of the organization, not everybody knew the CEO well. Not everybody knew what to expect. As I spoke I could feel some lack of belief in the room, "Here it comes, one more initiative, one more buzzword, one more program of the month, yadda, yadda, yadda..."

Who can blame them? Healthcare is loaded with initiatives, movements, and programs that end up over budget, late, and underperforming. The issue is often not the plan, not the software, not the goal, and not the steps to achieve the result. It most often is the lack of execution.

Years ago I was at an organization in which we hired a consultant to reengineer processes for $1.8 million; at the end of one year the consulting company offered to help us put things back the way they were before the reengineering. Another time in another organization we spent $1.4 million to reduce length of stay and decrease patient outliers. Several months later, after early gains, we were back where we started—except $1.4 million shorter.

While at the time I pointed fingers at others, in retrospect the issue was me. I did not make sure that everyone was on board, that an objective leader evaluation was in place, that leaders were trained in the skills needed to make necessary changes, that staff and physicians were totally in the loop in education and input, and that the "why" connection had been made.

Their experiences laid such a foundation for me to do what I can so others do not have to fail as I did. That is what this book and Studer Group are about: making healthcare better. Our vision is to be the place to turn when leaders and organizations want to improve performance. So much for self-disclosure! Let's get back to the perception of the question about the CEO being on board.

Anyway, people came up to me and asked, "What if Dr. B is not on board?" They were so busy worrying about him that I was concerned they were not thinking about what they needed to do. Isn't it always easier to figure out what somebody else should do than what you, yourself, should do?

So I gave the leaders an assignment. I said, "Many of you have come up to me and worried about what if Dr. B is not on board. Let's put the discussion on the table; too often we keep the issue buried or hidden." (Let me add that Dr. B was in the room and he knew where I was going with this.) I continued, "Your assignment today is to go home and write a paragraph titled *What Does 'On Board' Look Like Regarding Dr. B?* We're going to go over your answers first thing in the morning."

The next morning we collected the paragraphs and started discussing what the people wrote that being on board looks like. What was found out is that "on board" is a pretty vague term. In fact, to most of the leaders at this LDI, "on board" meant being more visible.

I said, "Well, that's a pretty weak definition—visible. Doesn't that mean if the CEO just walks up and down the hallways and is visible then he's on board?"

So we really started digging into what on board looks like.

Now, let's talk for a moment about visibility. Years ago the CEO of a multi-hospital system in Kentucky got the message from employees that being "on board" meant being more visible. So he figured out that if he visited every department in every hospital it would literally take him years to be as visible as they wanted him to. So he said, "I will not be as visible as you want me to be, but here's how visible I will be." He actually sent out his schedule for the next year on when he would be visiting each hospital and so on.

"On Board" Is about Commitment— and a Lot More.

Being "on board" is about action. It is about relentlessness in achieving desired results. It is about role modeling the standards of behavior agreed upon in the organization. It is about transparency, accountability, and admitting mistakes. It is about putting in systems that achieve and sustain outcomes that meet the organization's mission and hardwiring processes, tools, and techniques so that the organization continues to move forward even when leaders leave.

The phrase "on board" can mean different things to different people.

To me, on board means committing to an evaluation tool that is effective. Or it may mean being willing to make sure that people have the amount of training they need—and that you won't back off on it even if you take a few financial hits.

On board might mean making sure the organization hardwires and verifies those tools and techniques that evidence shows achieve better outcomes.

On board might mean living the Standards of Behavior your organization has identified. It might mean you are willing to deal with the low performers who are dragging everyone else down.

What I have discovered is that the CEO being on board is really not the issue. The real issue is getting everybody to own their own "on board ship" instead of worrying about somebody else being on board.

Little Things Can Make People Think You're Not On Board.

At a "Taking You and Your Organization to the Next Level" session, a group of employees came up to me. They asked me what they should do if the CEO is not living the values of the organization.

Well, to me that was a pretty strong statement. I didn't even know if I wanted to hear the rest of the story. Still, I asked, "What do you mean?"

And one of the men said, "Well, they tell us that we need to wear our name badges on our uniform at all times but the CEO walks around the hallway without his name badge."

I gave the CEO a call. Because I worked with the system, he knew that I talked to his corporate leaders all the time. I told him that I enjoyed having his people at the TYYO and then I added that some of them shared with me their concern that he does not live the values.

There was a great pause on his end, and then I said, "What they meant was you're not wearing your name badge."

Well, I think I felt a sigh of relief come over the phone. Then he basically said, "They are right. I've got two of them in my drawer right now. I will put one on and I will wear it from now on."

And I said, "If you can do one thing more for me, please tell people that you weren't wearing your name badge, that somebody brought it up to you, and that you are so appreciative and thankful for the reminder. Let the staff know that although you've tried to always live the standards and the values, you are only human. And if for any reason they think you're not doing so, you would really appreciate it if they would bring it to your attention."

I find most of the time people try to do the best job they can, but at times there are some misses. We have to get people feeling comfortable enough to tell us about it.

Here's another story about a "little thing" that doesn't seem so little to others. "Little" or "big" is in the eye of the beholder.

I was in another hospital in Tennessee and the security guard approached me and said, "We have parking rules and all of the managers and staff are supposed to park over there. The problem we have is that the president tends to pull up in front of the hospital and park in front of the overhang to go into his office.

"Now what that really does is cause a lot of problems," he added. "I'm trying to enforce the parking restrictions, and everybody says, 'Well, what about Mr. So-and-so?'"

Now, I know you might be thinking, *But he's coming and going. He's just stopping in for a minute and then he's leaving.*

My answer is this: It doesn't matter. Where you park has symbolic meaning and people do notice it.

When the CEO was made aware of the stress his forbidden parking spot was causing security, he started parking with the other hospital employees.

At the next LDI, he apologized and said it would not happen again. He told them he realized that was not a good example so he moved his car to park where everybody else parks. Actions such as these can make a big impact.

On Board Means Putting Others First.

Years ago in California, a group of nurses told me about the CEO at the hospital in which they worked. Mary Jo was the CEO's name. What she did is a classic illustration of the *Is the executive team on board?* question.

The hospital the nurses worked at was preparing to do some construction. They were going to expand one of the units and it just so happened that the Nursing Lounge was going to be taken out of play. The unit would have to go several months without a Nursing Lounge, so they thought.

The hospital brought a trailer in and people naturally assumed that it was going to be a construction trailer. Instead, the CEO moved Administration into the trailer, and then she took Administration's offices and turned them into the Nursing Lounge.

The CEO came to work the morning after the moves and there was a gift that all of the nurses had chipped in and bought her to say, "Thank you for thinking of us."

So how do senior leaders get on board? Well, we ask the people we work with to help explain what on board looks like. Then, we make sure we're really straight on what we can and cannot do. Next, we put it in writing.

When I was at Holy Cross Hospital, CEO Mark Clement had us put together a written commitment from senior leadership. He had us to create a Senior Leaders Standards of Behavior document that was a bit tougher than the standards everyone else followed.

That's a good start. Also, ask people to let you know if they catch you not being on board. If they seem to be afraid of you, ask them what you can do to make yourself more approachable.

To close out this chapter, I was talking to a new CEO one day and she told me that she had a hard time getting people to disagree with her. Well, after talking to this CEO, I could see that she was a little intense. I could understand why people would be hesitant at first to maybe bring up problems to her.

So I asked her if people ever disagreed with her privately in her own office. She said yes.

I said, "I think I see what the protocol is in your organization. If I'm going to disagree with the boss, I'm not to do it in public. See, right now you're in public forums and trying to inspire all this debate, all this healthy conversation, but nobody knows that the rules have changed. They are a little afraid of what will happen."

She wanted to know what she should do about it.

I said, "Next time you're in a private meeting and somebody questions you, ask him to hold that question and to bring it up at the next department meeting. Then, when he does, compliment him on bringing it up and answer the question.

"In fact, it's even better if you can change where you are on the issue," I told her. "If the person says, 'I don't think that is a good idea and we should do this instead,' you can actually change your stance. That will show staff members that not only is it okay to question you; you will actually adjust your thinking based on more relevant information."

SUMMARY

Working in healthcare is not easy. Often, it is not comfortable. Being a leader adds additional responsibilities; it is not for the weak-kneed or faint-hearted.

It seems that just about the time a leader gets it figured out, either we are at the age of retirement or the environment changes so we have to learn and make more adjustments.

It is my hope that we can continue to learn from each other. One of the best aspects of leadership in healthcare is that leaders and organizations willingly share ways to get better. We put competition to the side. We know it is not what one knows but how one executes.

The exercises in this chapter get to the heart of execution: a team with eyes wide open, with the ability to self-assess performance, with the understanding that discomfort (tension) comes with improved performance, and with the ability to connect the dots back to the "why."

SECTION FOUR:

THE BASICS

To create a "Straight A" organization, leaders must follow certain overarching leadership principles and techniques.

In Section 1 we covered what needs to happen in order to adapt to the demands of a changing external environment. Now, we'll touch on some of the ways we can *make* it happen.

The topics covered in Section 4 are:
- A Word about Consistency
- Align the Organization into Pillars (Components) of Excellence
- Focus on "Basics" (the Skills Leaders Need)
- Adopt Leader Evaluations That Work
- Move Best Practices Throughout the Organization
- Implement High/Middle/Low Conversations
- Connect Employees to Why
- Heal We/They Divisiveness

There is always more to learn. However, by absorbing the ideas in this book and applying its principles, tools, and techniques, you and your organization will be better able to weather the ever-changing external environment.

CHAPTER FIFTEEN:

A WORD ABOUT CONSISTENCY

I n a way this entire book is about consistency. In fact, the first word in the subtitle—*Alignment*—conveys how critical it is that leaders speak in the same voice, follow the same processes and procedures, embrace the same practices, and work to achieve the same outcomes. It's what enables physicians and staff to have the best places to make a difference.

Cross-organizational consistency leads to sustainable results. It ensures that all patients and families have the best possible experience. It ensures that all employees have excellent leaders. It allows the hiring of the right employees and creates loyalty. It creates the organization's brand.

Of course, consistency isn't *just* the realm of leaders. It applies to everyone associated with organizations, from physicians to employees at every level. But because leaders set, model, and manage the policies everyone lives by, they are truly the organization's Ambassadors of Consistency.

That said, standardizing leader behavior is a critical part of hardwiring consistency into your organization. As we discussed in Chapter 4, many leaders balk at sharing their best practices—and many others don't seek out and embrace the best practices of their colleagues.

Many of the "basics" covered in this chapter will help to reduce leader variances. Many of the tools in the last section of the book serve this purpose as well.

Still, I wanted to provide a quick "CliffsNotes" version to help you get started:

1. Use a common agenda. Studer Group recommends the Five Pillars of Excellence—People, Service, Quality, Finance, and Growth—as an organizing model, goal-setting foundation, and meeting agenda. (If you have a sixth pillar, Community is the most often used one.) Whether you use it or some other model, it gives leaders throughout the organization a standardized "home base" from which to work. This approach aligns all staff to the same goals and connects them to the organization's mission and vision. It also provides a single mechanism to cascade information to staff.

2. Align the evaluation process to the pillars or the organization's critical success factors. Make sure

goals are objective, measurable, meaningful, aligned, and focused on results.

3. Ensure that each leader leaves every department meeting with a packet of information to share with staff so that every employee hears the same information.

4. Choose a single common selection method for hiring purposes. All applicants should be asked at least two or three of the same behavioral-based questions geared toward values and ownership regardless of the job for which they are interviewing.

5. Collect from leaders the tough questions heard from staff. Work with leaders to develop ways to respond uniformly across the organization when questions are asked. Teach leaders to also play offense in asking about items before others do.

6. Make sure all leaders have been trained in basic competencies to use the above five tactics.

Measurement is another important aspect of consistency. The ability to objectively assess the current status and track the progress to the goals set is what lets departments that are falling short be quickly identified. You can then zero-in on problem areas and bring them up to speed to the higher performing areas. Also, solid, objective metrics form the basis of leader evaluations and allow for evaluations on performance versus personalities.

A full discussion of all the elements that make up organizational consistency is beyond the scope of this book. *Straight A Leadership* is not intended to be an exhaustive "how to" manual. Still, the topics that follow connect back to the diagnostics we discussed in the first four chapters of this book—which, together, provide a helpful framework for infusing consistency into your organization.

Align the Organization into Pillars (Components) of Excellence.

Every organization needs a foundation for setting goals. When Studer Group works with clients, we often recommend that they use a model we call The Five Pillars of Excellence. We find that the pillar model provides consistency and focus over time and helps organizations resist "fad" programs that may tempt them to veer off course.

In other words, the Five Pillars help organizations avoid straying away from a key goal. They keep an organization grounded. They also help each person see how the work they do impacts the organization. Every employee will be able to see how his or her job impacts at least one part of each pillar. This is what separates the framework from a program or an initiative.

Studer Group adapted the model from Clay Sherman's wonderful book *Creating the New American Hospital: A Time for Greatness* (John Wiley & Sons, 1993).

Specifically, we added a fifth pillar (which I define as Growth, or access) and moved "cost" within a new Finance Pillar, which better describes financial goals for us. Clay's work connected the dots for me.

Together, the Five Pillars provide a foundation for the Three As. This model helps leaders stay aligned in setting organizational goals and take action toward a balanced array of short- and long-term objectives. It also creates a framework for an evaluation process that holds leaders accountable, since all leaders are evaluated against established metrics under each pillar.

Below is an example of one organization's use of the Five Pillars:

Pillar Framework

Service	Quality	People
• Reduced claims • Reduced legal expenses • Reduced malpractice expenses • Physician Satisfaction • Patient Satisfaction	• Improved clinical outcomes - decreased nosocomial infections • Reduced medically unnecessary days and delays • Reduced re-admits • Reduced medication errors	• Reduced turnover • Reduced vacancies • Reduced agency costs • Reduced overtime • Reduced physicals and cost to orient

Finance	Growth	Community
• Improved operating income • Decreased cost per adjusted discharge • Improved collections • Reduced accounts receivable days • Reduced advertising costs	• Higher volume • Increased revenue • Decreased left without treatment in the ED • Reduced outpatient no-shows • Increased physician activity	• Increased philanthropy

StuderGroup▼

Figure 15.1: Pillar Framework

Pillar Goals Work in Synergy.

What do goals look like under the Five Pillars? Here are a few examples of typical "start-up" goals. (Obviously, the goals will change as the organization matures.)

Service—Achieve average percentile ranking of patient satisfaction on hospital survey greater than 95th percentile

Quality—Reduce incidence of hospital-acquired skin-pressure ulcers to 2.4 percent or less

People—Reduce average employee turnover to 12 percent or less

Finance—Increase annual operating income margin to 4 percent or greater

Growth—Increase outpatient visits 6 percent or greater over previous year

Community—Increase philanthropy and giving by 5 percent or greater

When goals are set up, it is apparent that the pillars work in synergy. Take the skin-pressure ulcer goal under Quality, for instance. Five percent of patients will acquire these ulcers during an inpatient stay, and they are very costly to healthcare organizations. Therefore, better prevention will result in substantial cost reduction under the Finance Pillar.

How do you achieve this goal? Well, one way is to better support employees by recognizing and rewarding their prevention efforts. When employees see how their efforts make a difference, employee satisfaction rises and turnover drops (People). Since improved quality comes with increased physician satisfaction, physicians refer more patients and create greater volume (Growth) and higher revenues (Finance) for the hospital. Also, patients will feel better about their care (Service).

Interestingly, the Service Pillar may be the last to yield measurable results due to handoffs during care. This means everyone needs to be very good. However, those results *will* come. And when patient satisfaction (or patient perception of care) improves, there are fewer claims and lower malpractice costs.

Ultimately, improvements made under every pillar translate to bottom-line results. For organizations striving to stay viable in a stormy external environment, that's very good news indeed.

Focus on "Basics" (the Skills Leaders Need)

Why do leaders choose to lead? And why do "interim" leaders stay in their positions? I think it's because they have a passion for improving, not only themselves but the organization as a whole. They want to expand their impact in their department and in the organization. For all the challenges that come with taking on a leadership role, there's no better way to impact as many people as possible.

Individuals without knowledge of the fundamentals of leadership are easily overwhelmed by their new job. They can't deal with everything going on in their external environment because they are struggling just to stay afloat.

These new leaders may have passion. But they don't know how to hire. They don't know how to read a budget or manage finances. They don't know how to fire. They are so busy just trying to survive that they don't have a chance to understand and learn what makes their internal environment tick, much less adapt to a changing external environment.

The Fundamentals of Leadership can provide managers with the foundation they need to be successful. We owe it to our leaders to train them in basic leadership skills.

Basic Leadership Skills
The Foundation

Leaders must be skilled in:

- Running effective meetings
- Managing financial resources
- Answering tough questions so as to not create a "we/they" culture (compensation including salaries)
- Selection of talent
- Development of talent
- Critical thinking
- De-selection
- *Understanding the external environment*
- Managing up the positive, the solution, and the decision

StuderGroup

Figure 15.2: Basic Leadership Skills -The Foundation

From working with organizations across the country, here are some techniques that we have found work well in training and developing leaders.

Three Steps to Creating Great Leaders

1) Hold Leadership Development Institutes (LDIs). LDIs give you an opportunity to get all of your leaders together. At your LDIs you can help all of your leaders get on the same page, communicate information to them as a whole group, and create a networking opportunity for them. Of course, in today's world, where you might have employees spread from Hawaii to Miami, it might be impossible to get them all together physically for an LDI, but you can still get them together virtually through webinars or virtual training programs. No matter what method you use, you'll find bringing your leaders together provides a valuable training opportunity that will greatly benefit them and your organization.

2) Focus on outcomes. Make sure people understand that the point isn't to get trained, but the outcomes that result from the training. It doesn't matter if everyone enjoyed the training session if 90 days later they are still getting the same results. Make sure people understand why they are being developed and focus them on specific outcomes.

If leaders are being trained on how to do a better job of hiring, the desired outcome should be less turnover, particularly less first-year turnover. If leaders are being trained and educated on financial stewardship, it is so they can be more productive and more effective. If leaders are being trained in physician satisfaction, it is so they can provide better services to physicians in order to achieve shorter length of stay by helping the physicians to move patients through more quickly. If the physicians are more satisfied with the services and care, their utilization of that hospital will increase.

> The bottom line: When training leaders always focus on the improved results the training is designed to achieve. Be very clear that you aren't training for the sake of training. Determine the outcome you want first—then match the training to it.

3) Follow up on the training in the supervisory sessions. Follow-up after a training session is key. Too often, there's not post-training follow-up, and the result is that those things that were talked about in training are never implemented successfully. Somehow it is the trainer's job. Development and training is just the beginning; the repetition of the skill is what creates the habits that lead to improved performance. Here's what a manager can say to a trainee during a follow-up conversation:

"Rick, at the last training session, a lot of time was devoted to peer interviewing, behavioral-based questioning, developing and using selection matrixes to pick the best job candidates, and implementing an on boarding process that includes 30- and 90-day interview questions.

"Rick, when you started this process, your turnover rate was 13 percent. Since you've been through training, tell me what systems you've put in place in order to ask better behavioral-based interview questions. And what are the questions you and your staff have selected?

"Tell me how you trained your peers. Tell me how you are verifying the 30- and 90-day meetings and walk me through how you chose your latest hires.

"Review the current results and what you feel they can be and when. What are you finding is working? Are there barriers you are encountering? If yes, let's discuss possible solutions."

Good leaders take ownership of the team by following up with and mentoring managers after training sessions. Otherwise, the changes that Human Resources or the chief learning officer are driving to deal with the external environment won't get implemented effectively.

The harsh reality in healthcare is that when times get tough, reimbursement decreases. And that's when many organizations say to their leaders, "Okay, it's a tougher environment, it's harder than ever to be successful—and by the way, we're going to provide less training."

In my book *Hardwiring Excellence*, I wrote that the way to tell if an organization is value-driven is to look at the amount of training leaders are provided. If people are to do a good job, they must be invested in. If we want leaders to take action, we've got to give them the skills, training, and experience to do so. The presence of undeveloped leaders creates an anxiety that is not healthy for them, their families, the staff, and the organization as a whole.

If someone doesn't feel he has the skills to take action, it does not happen. In order to get results, organizations have to commit to skill development in leaders to a greater extent than they've ever done before...yes, even in tough times. Maybe even more so.

Adopt Leader Evaluations That Work.

How effective are your leader evaluations? Are individuals evaluated based on personality or on performance? Do the evaluations motivate leaders to focus on the issues that matter most to the organization? And do they hold leaders accountable for results?

We've always known that how people are evaluated has a big impact on how they perform. But in an era defined by a rapidly changing external environment, the issue takes on new significance. Leaders have to do their best possible work, and direct their focus to the right areas, if an organization is to remain nimble and competitive. Leadership agility equals organization agility, which is vital for today's (and tomorrow's) environment.

If you're convinced that your evaluation tool isn't serving you like it should, you may be wondering where to turn next. What does a good evaluation tool look like, anyway? And how should you be evaluating your leaders? At Studer Group, our research and experience show:

1) A good evaluation tool should be objective—the more objective, the better. The reason is simple: Subjective measurement leads to people being judged on personality rather than performance. But *can* a leader

evaluation tool be 100 percent objective? We have found that the answer is yes, but some organizations just aren't comfortable with that ideal. At minimum, 80 percent of it should be objective.

2) If possible, avoid evaluations that rate employees on a "meet," "does not meet," and "exceeds" scale. A five-point system is preferable. It gives you a more precise measurement of performance. It also makes being a high performer a little bit tougher. We find that 70 percent of all leaders usually have an evaluation that identifies them as high performers no matter what the performance of the organization is. We recommend a 1 through 5 rating with 3 being the goal, 4 being above the goal and 5 being far above the goal. (Of course, 2 means below goal and 1 means the leader really missed it.)

3) No leader should be held accountable for more than 10 goals. The fewer goals someone is being held accountable for the better. We have found that more than 10 goals per leader starts diluting results.

Of course, leaders in different departments can have different goals. What they will have in common is that the goals are objective and weighted to reflect their relative importance to the performance of a particular leader.

The CNO might have a goal of improving clinical quality while the ER manager might have a goal of reducing the number of patients who leave without being treated. The good news about reducing the left-without-being-treated component is that it positively impacts admission and shows up on the bottom line. It usually shows up somewhere on a CEO or C-Suite leader's evaluation but not in as specific a way as it does the manager's. So it's important to come up with objective measurements that best fit each leader.

Prioritization: Why It Matters

Organizations that want to better respond to changes in the external environment will want to prioritize their evaluation goals. The idea is to focus leaders on what they need to do to achieve the desired outcomes.

Let's say one external environment change is that a physician group has opened up an outpatient diagnostic center in your area. It has pulled away CTs, MRIs, and radiology work that used to be done in your organization. You will want to modify the evaluation of the head of imaging to make the Growth Pillar a high priority.

Often, a CEO will tell us that the organization really needs to focus on growth. Yet we find that growth is not a key component on the evaluations of most of the organization's managers. Many managers simply say they can't impact growth directly (in the same way that, for instance, a one-day surgery center manager can), so that particular goal is weighted very lightly on their evaluations.

Weighted goals allow the CEO to make sure leaders are working on what they should be working on, to the extent that they need to be working on it. A 30 percent weight would create a sense of urgency in a manager, a

20 percent weight would lead to focus, and a 10 percent weight simply means it will not be forgotten or ignored. (More on this shortly.)

However, every manager can have some control over growth, in an indirect way. Better service, better physician relations, reduction of no-shows, regular call backs, increased efficiency, and so on—all lead to better patient satisfaction and thus promote growth.

Get Leaders Focused by Weighting Their Goals.

Now, let's look at where we want individual leaders to focus. When we talk to leaders across the country about what they want from their senior leaders, here is what they say: *Tell me* specifically *what you want me to accomplish; help me with priorities;* and *give me the training and coaching I need in order to do it.*

Weighting goals is what allows leaders to meet this request. We don't recommend that every goal be given the same percentage of importance. Instead, it's best to place weight exactly where you want a specific individual to focus.

Dave Fox, CEO of Advocate Good Samaritan in Downers Grove, Illinois, and his team really understand prioritization. Year after year his organization leads the country in clinical outcomes as well as other measures. His evaluation process shows his managers truly understand what's most important.

A couple of years ago when they wanted to reduce central line infections and hospital-acquired pneumonia, he went into his managers' evaluation area in the ICU and aligned them to accomplish just that. In fact, he made it so that a high percentage of their evaluation was based on quality goals of reducing central line infections and eliminating hospital-acquired pneumonia.

Interestingly, the patient satisfaction goal had a low weighting. It's not that patient satisfaction was not important. It's that the CEO was fairly confident that this matter would be taken care of before and after the patient's ICU stay. He wanted the ICU to put an increased focus on ventilator-associated pneumonia and ICU central line blood infections. As you can see by the graphs, his strategy succeeded.

Not only did this hospital improve clinical care in its ICU, the financial impact was significant, with more than $400,000 saved due to decrease of central line infections and more than $500,000 saved due to decrease in ventilator days and ventilator-associated pneumonia. Most importantly, think of the lives that were saved.

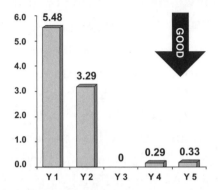

ICU Ventilator-Associated Pneumonia

ICU Ventilator-Associated Pneumonia
Per 1,000 ventilator days

Source: Advocate Good Samaritan Hospital, Downers Grove, Illinois
Beds=320, Admissions=18,300; 2004-2008

StuderGroup

Figure 15.3: Weighted Evaluation Result - ICU Ventilator-Associated Pneumonia

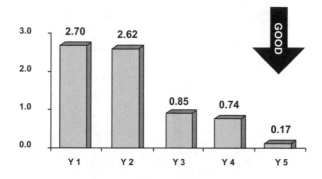

Figure 15.4: Weighted Evaluation Result - ICU Central
Line Blood Stream Infections

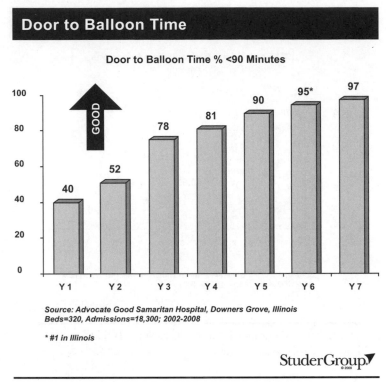

Figure 15.5: Weighted Evaluation Result – Door to Balloon Time

Goals like patient satisfaction would be a priority in, for example, the Emergency Department. After all, it's what reduces the number of patients who leave without being seen.

Align the organization's prioritization to what you, the C-Suite, want your department directors, managers, and supervisors to see as the most important for their area. This determination is very much dependent on the external environment, of course. Studer Group has over 50,000 examples of evaluations for leaders using the above format.

To view sample evaluation goals and metrics, visit www.studergroup.com/StraightALeadership.

A Sample "Focusing" Tactic: Key Words at Key Times

Once a department has been given a particular focus, how do its leaders turn that focus into action? The answer depends on what they're trying to accomplish, of course, but we at Studer Group have found there are certain predictable tools and tactics that have a positive impact in a variety of arenas and situations.

Here is an example. We worked with one organization that wanted to improve its cash on hand. So it told relevant managers that they would be held accountable for co-pay collections in their evaluations. The evaluation was adjusted and then it adopted the "key words at key times" tactic, which can also be called AIDET[SM], in its Admitting and Registration Departments. See Figure 15.6.

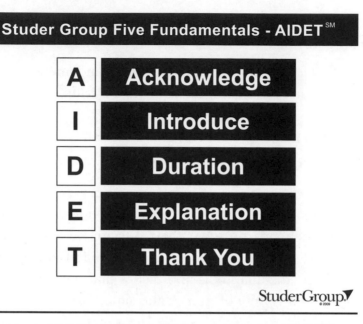

Figure 15.6: Studer Group Five Fundamentals - AIDET^{SM}

You're probably familiar with the use of AIDET in the clinical arena. Most likely you associate it with patient satisfaction. But as this example clearly shows, AIDET is just as effective in the financial realm. Simply by teaching the staff the impact of key words during patient interactions, this organization enjoyed measurable financial improvement.

Here is what staff members were asked to say:

"Mrs. Jones, my name is Dan and I work in Patient Registration as a patient financial representative for the hospital. I would like to provide you with your insurance benefit coverage for your upcoming service. This will take only a few minutes of your time. Your insurance has been verified. Your insurance requires you to pay a co-pay in the amount of $25.00. How would you like to pay that today? Cash, check, or credit card..."

As Figure 15.7 clearly shows, the hospital's co-pays went way up. Simply by getting the leaders and staff focused on upfront collections, it saw dramatic financial results in the first six months and continues to see increases in year two.

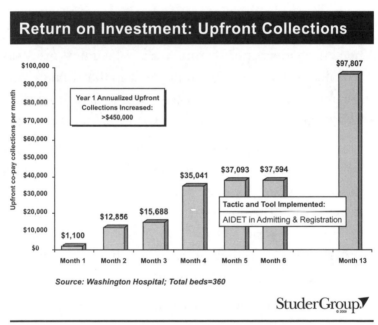

Return on Investment: Upfront Collections

Year 1 Annualized Upfront Collections Increased: >$450,000

Tactic and Tool Implemented: AIDET in Admitting & Registration

Source: Washington Hospital; Total beds=360

StuderGroup

Figure 15.7: Financial Impact – Co-pay and Upfront Collection Increase

To access Studer Group's AIDET tools, please visit www.studergroup.com/StraightALeadership.

You can see getting focused on the right things really matters in the face of the changing external environment. It's more critical than ever that we have the best possible system for evaluating people, holding them accountable, and setting priorities for them. This also creates the opportunity to connect the collections to how the money is used to provide better patient care. It lets us make that important connection back to the "why."

Move Best Practices Throughout the Organization.

As a rule, healthcare organizations aren't great at moving best practices. The data shows it. We just aren't. When one leader is performing well, colleagues rarely say, "We'd like to start doing whatever it is that makes your department so successful. Will you tell us your secret?" And the leader rarely volunteers the information either.

For a variety of reasons (which we explored in Chapter 4), people naturally resist asking for help or pushing their way of doing things on someone else. That's too bad, because standardizing best practices and applying them throughout the organization can make organizations far more effective and efficient, save significant amounts of money, and generate tremendous revenue.

Obviously, in a tough external environment, all of these are desirable outcomes.

Take a Cue from Non-Healthcare Organizations.

Due to my book *Results That Last* and its "general business" readership, I've spoken to many non-healthcare organizations over the years. I've found that non-healthcare organizations

> are better at transferring learning outside
> their area and I believe the reason is simple:
> Their competitors *won't* share best practices.
> Therefore, employees relate to their cowork-
> ers in terms of "it's us against the world"
> rather than "it's my department against your
> department."

Many companies even have contractual terms that prevent people from sharing preferred practices if they leave that organization. For example, if you're working in an IT company, your competition isn't going to tell you its latest programming technique. Or if you're part of a hotel chain and you're trying to improve the hotel's level of service, a competing hotel chain isn't going to say, "Hey, let me show you what we've done."

Non-healthcare companies and industries have had to learn to transfer best practices. In fact, when I present our techniques to non-healthcare employees, they are much more receptive than many healthcare employees. They say, "Even though these methods are used mainly in healthcare, they'll work for us too. We can round on our employees. We can do 30- and 90-day interviews. We can do pre-calls. We can do call backs. Yep, we need a better evaluation tool."

An Example of Moving Best Practices

Healthcare organizations must learn to transfer best practices as well as their non-healthcare counter-parts. And it's a matter of learning to relate instead of comparing. How do you relate to another department? Here's an example:

When I was working at Baptist Hospital in Pensacola, we had a number of nurses who were not keeping up to date with their continuing education credits. We had a rule that you could not get your evaluation until you were caught up. Eventually everybody *would* be caught up, but in the meantime people were being evaluated at different times and pay raises were being given at different times. And all of the back and forth with pay adjustments was becoming problematic.

One day I got a note from Terry Wood, a nurse manager of the Surgical Intensive Care Unit. Terry asked me to send a thank-you note to one of her employees thanking her for doing such a good job of making sure all of the nurses kept up to date with their continuing education units to maintain their nursing certification. In her unit, everyone was up to date.

Well, as I was writing this note, I found myself really wanting to know how this lady did it. When I visited Terry, she told me that every 90 days a nurse was in charge of making sure everyone was up to date with his or her continuing education credits. She had found that a peer asking this question worked better than a leader asking it. It also allowed every nurse to take ownership of the unit at some point.

There was also give and take between the nurses because they knew that while one person might be asking them about their credits this month, next month they would be the one in charge of asking. Knowing that created a sense of cooperation. Long story short, we ended up implementing that unit's system throughout the entire organization. We solved the payroll issues. Everyone kept up to date, and it became a standard practice.

How to Harvest and Standardize Best Practices

Harvesting best practices is necessary. Just look at the metrics and don't get caught up in the "oh, we're so different" mentality. The key is to relate, not to compare. I've been in a 25-bed hospital and I've been in a 1,000-bed hospital and I'm not saying they are exactly alike, but I am saying they're more alike than they are different. So the same harvesting procedure that works in one place will probably work in another.

When a leader starts getting or gets and sustains solid results, take time to assess exactly what his or her best practice is and then follow the steps necessary for spreading it throughout the organization.

Here's how:

1) Diagnose what is being done. Carefully research any change in processes, tools, techniques, and, just as importantly, leader behavior.

2) Take time to **document your findings.**

3) Create a Best Practice Transfer Manual that outlines outcomes and processes and provides a list of possible Q & As. The manual will help ease push back because it will make implementing the best practice easier for everyone involved. In the manual **spell out and sequence the steps necessary** for successfully implementing the best practice. Doing so will help avoid overwhelming employees with the new way of doing things, which often leads to transfer failure.

4) Assess the skills needed to implement the best practice. The person who created or originally implemented the best practice may have some skills that others do not. Assess what skills are needed in order for other organization leaders to implement the practice successfully. Can the best practice still be implemented if the leader in place does not have the skills? You may need to decide whether his department should just keep going business as usual and not implement the new best practice, or you may realize you need to replace that leader. Or go to step 5.

5) Get training in place for leaders. Obviously, training those leaders who will be teaching others how to implement the best practice is crucial. Be sure that no stone goes unturned and don't unleash your leaders to start teaching their employees until you are certain that they all know exactly what they should be doing.

6) Establish a firm plan for those who lack the will or the skill. A leader might have the skill to implement a best practice, but does she have the will? Another leader might have plenty of will, but does he have the skill? Without one or the other, you are going to run into problems implementing the best practice. But where both are present, success is sure to follow. When you see that a leader is lacking one or the other, ask yourself, *Can he acquire the other element needed? How fast can he acquire it? At what cost?* Then decide if the time and cost are worth the investment. If you feel it is not, then it might be time to remove or demote that leader.

7) Identify the "why" and keep in front of the organization. In healthcare when changes are made, it's for a reason. Make sure your employees understand this. It's imperative that they know the "why" behind the implementation of the best practice. Is it to improve care and save more lives? Is it to provide better access to help more people? Is it to lower expenses? In healthcare the "why" drives the "what" so make sure the "why" is clear for everyone involved.

8) Hold people accountable for results. Naturally, the best practice is meant to improve performance. If you aren't seeing the desired outcomes from your leaders and their employees, then you need to hold those individuals accountable. If you let their mediocre results slide, the best practice will be looked at as an option and will likely not be optimized.

9) Put in validation systems. Tools that validate implementation are critical to measure implementation. For example, if you're standardizing 30- and 90-day meetings with new employees to reduce turnover and you don't have a system to validate the necessary steps taking place, you will not get to the critical mass to have the maximum success. You will also miss all of the performance improvement techniques in the validation process. If you don't validate, you won't get the consistency you need to get the desired outcome. So trust but verify.

10) Recognize those departments that are doing well in implementation. When the other departments see that the new behavior is being recognized and commended, they will move to that behavior. Use meetings, emails, letters, and other avenues to spotlight those departments or individuals who are doing a great job with the new best practice or to announce when milestones are reached. Remember, recognize early and often! If you're waiting until your employees have all reached the ultimate goal to recognize a job well done, then you may never get there.

11) Standardize the steps. Make sure everyone in the organization becomes very familiar with the steps in order to standardize the best practice. Make those steps consistent. It will be much easier for you to implement future best practices successfully.

> Standardization can be tough for some executives. In healthcare today, we standardize many things: supply chain management, temperature control, parking in such a way that parking stickers can be easily seen. All kinds of behaviors, tools, and processes are

standardized except for, ironically, the one that matters the most—leadership.

Studer Group works with three hospitals that are part of an eight-hospital system. The three hospitals we work with have tremendous performance levels, but the other five hospitals in the system won't implement our best practices because it's not their thing. The excuses are much like those we discussed earlier. But it really shouldn't matter what they are. There comes a time when the CEO just has to say, "This system works, or this procedure or this tool works, and we're going to standardize it. Period."

12) Keep searching. There is no shortage of better ways to do things in healthcare, nor is there a lack of desire to share. A great characteristic of healthcare is the willingness of organizations to teach and learn from each other. While there will always be differences, the similarities far outweigh them. Never stop searching for the next great way to do something.

13) Don't get too hung up on *best*. When I worked for him at Holy Cross Hospital in Chicago, Illinois, Mark Clement taught me that if it is better than what is taking place, then go for better. We can worry about *best* after *better*.

Implement High/Middle/Low Performer Conversations.

When an organization is struggling to survive an economic hurricane, all employees must perform at the absolute top of their games. This is critical. There is no room for mediocrity, and there's certainly no room for outright poor performance.

In Chapter 2, we discussed the necessity for dealing with low performers. Leaders must move these individuals up or out. At the same time, we must re-recruit the men and women on the other end of the spectrum and push the large group in the middle to improve their performances as well.

High, Middle, and Low Performer Conversations allow leaders to do just that.

Re-Recruit High Performers.

Let's start by looking at high performers. You know who these people are. They thrive on achievement. They don't need a lot of supervision and in fact generally pride themselves on not needing to be supervised. It should go without saying that these are the people you want to keep—especially in tough economic times. That's why it's so important to re-recruit them.

High performers tend to focus on achievement. However, if there is one place in which high performers need help, it is in recognizing the impact they can have on other people. High achievers are so focused on their own performances they might not naturally help or mentor someone else. However, when asked to focus on mentoring, they excel. They immediately turn themselves into excellent helpers.

What do high performers need? They want to be with winning organizations, organizations that are clearly moving in the right direction. When you round, make these points to your high performers. Tell them that you know that the organization is moving in the right direction. Be specific. These people have high expectations of themselves, so they want an organization that has high expectations of itself.

> Be careful not to generalize with high performers. Don't go into a room with 50 people and say, "You all do a great job." Why? Because the real high performers in the room will look around and see that not everyone there truly *does* do a great job. High performers do better with one-on-one coaching and with feedback that is specific to them only.

High performers often underestimate their importance. Let's say you go up to a great hitter in baseball—Ted Williams, perhaps—and you ask, "Can you teach me how to hit a baseball like you?"

His response might be: "Well, it's pretty simple. You just watch the number of stitches, and you hit the ball."

Well, Ted Williams had 20/10 eyesight. He might have been able to see the stitches, but not only would most of us *not* be able to see the stitches, we would have a rough time even making out the fast-approaching ball!

In other words, with high performers, be very specific about what they bring to the table because they might be underestimating the significance of their impacts and influence. Let them know you appreciate their work, thank them, and outline exactly what they do that is so valuable for the organization.

Next, ask high performers what you can do to keep them. Nine times out of ten, you'll find that high performers won't ask for money. They will ask for more training. They will ask for more responsibility or more opportunity. High performers want to improve. Their motivation to be the best is more of a driver for them than money.

Develop Middle Performers.

Who are your middle performers? They make up the majority of the workforce. They actually do a pretty good job most of the time. In fact, sometimes they do an excellent job, but the difference between them and high performers is consistency. It could just be experience. It could be the level of mentorship they've had in the past. Or it could be natural ability; things just come naturally to some people that don't come naturally to others.

While high performers transfer learning quite well— i.e., figuring out the material they've been trained in and translating it to action—middle performers often need someone with greater understanding to explain it to them. Middle performers are quite teachable. (Low performers, whom we'll address shortly, don't want to be taught.)

In fact, the reason so many healthcare organizations neglect to perform leadership training as often as they should is because they have so many leaders who do exceptionally well without it. Decision makers fall into the trap of thinking, *Well, if they can do without training, why do these other individuals need it?* It's because 58 percent of people don't transfer learning well. They need it transferred for them.

What do middle performers need in order to become high performers? They need personal connections with leaders who say, "We care about how well you do." They need to know they are appreciated. They need leaders who make sure they have the systems and tools to do the job well. They are not as good as high performers at coming up with solutions to problems on their own, so it's important to have their work environment as stabilized and solid as possible.

> Also, leaders should let their middle performers know they want to keep them because these employees actually worry about their job security more than the high or low performers. Why? Because high performers know they do a good job and thus feel secure. And low performers figure if they have lasted this long, they are safe.

Middle performers have more anxiety. Leaders should make it clear to these employees that they are important parts of the team. When you meet with a middle performer, identify what she does well. Be very specific about which of her skills you appreciate. Then pick one professional development item on which she needs to work.

According to Franklin/Covey research, if people work on one behavioral change, they will be much more successful. But ask them to make too many changes at once, and it becomes more difficult for them to succeed. So keep the focus on one area in which the middle performer can improve. These employees want to know their leaders are committed to their development.

At the end of your conversations with middle performers, sum up everything discussed, the skills they have, the value they bring to the organization, and the characteristics they bring to the job. Doing this will help you show them just how appreciated they are. It will make them feel good about what they are doing at the organization and will motivate them to improve in the area discussed during the meeting.

To access tools and articles related to highmiddlelow®, please visit www.studergroup.com/StraightALeadership.

Move Low Performers Up or Out.

Low performers probably make up 8 percent of the average workforce. Unfortunately, they tend to take up a huge amount of a manager's time. Left unchecked, they will drag middle performers down to their level and drive high performers out the door. (High performers hate working with these people.) It is absolutely imperative to address performance issues.

The low performer conversations are by far the most difficult. That's because these individuals are much more experienced with difficult conversations than the leader could ever hope to be. Many low performers have survived several supervisors by developing survival skills that most leaders haven't even considered.

These survival skills include blaming others for their poor performance, pointing the finger at their direct supervisors, or using a personal problem as an excuse. I've had good managers walk away from their conversations with low performers convinced that *they*, not the low performers, have been the problems all along!

It's best if managers practice and role play the low performer conversations with their bosses before talking with the low performers. Also before the conversations, managers should go to Human Resources to see what their options are. Don't assume HR won't let you take action with this person because of lack of documentation. Even though your records are not as organized as you'd like, HR might allow you to go further than you expect.

For the best outcome, use the D-E-S-K Approach for low performer conversations. Here's how it goes:

Describe the poor performance.
Evaluate processes, steps, procedures, and standards not followed.
Show what needs to be done and how.
Know the consequences of continued low performance.

The conversation needs to be direct and the tone firm. Set deadlines for improvement and follow up relentlessly.

One-third of the low performers will take the conversation to heart and will improve their performance. Another third will quit rather than change. However, the final third will simply try to wait you out and will eventually have to be let go. Studer Group research has shown that no low performers will improve or deselect themselves until at least one low performer is terminated.

As difficult and unpleasant as a firing can be, the firing will remove a tremendous obstacle to change from a department. More than likely, the other employees will be thrilled and the overall performance for the department will increase, even though everyone has to work harder until the position is filled.

Please note: Usually, there are performance issues in all parts of the organization. The higher up in an organization a performance issue is, the more damage will be done. It is particularly important to deal with high-ranking low performers quickly and decisively. In a harsh external environment, organizations simply can't afford not to.

Connect Employees to "Why."

If you know Studer Group, you're probably familiar with our Healthcare Flywheel®. It appears on the covers of many of the books we publish and is a focal point in many of our educational materials. When we present the flywheel, we always make a dotted line from the words in the center—Purpose, worthwhile work, and making a difference—that directs the eye outward to the word "Why."

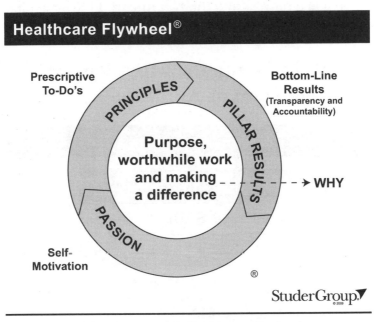

Figure 15.8: Studer Group® Healthcare Flywheel

On the surface, this "why" refers to the leader's need to explain why a certain decision was made. ("The department can't have a new copier because revenue is down and there is a freeze on all spending that doesn't directly impact patient care.") That's the first level of "why," the level that eliminates the we/they disconnect and positions the organization as a unified whole.

But let's look deeper. Beneath the surface of the facts-and-figures explanation is an opportunity for leaders to connect with employees on why what they do needs to be done and why it is important to the organization and the patients they serve. It connects them back to purpose, worthwhile work, and making a difference—which is, of course, the big picture "why."

To learn more about the Healthcare Flywheel, please visit www.studergroup.com/StraightALeadership.

"Why" Taps into the Most Powerful Leverage Point of All: Values.

Leverage Points in an Organization

Values
Skill
Recognition
Consequences
Money

StuderGroup▼

Figure 15.9: Leverage Points in an Organization

There are various "leverage points" leaders can use to inspire and influence people when trying to change their behaviors. One of them is skill. When people don't have the skills they need, leaders can make sure they get them. Another leverage point is recognition. Many times, when people see other people being recognized, it inspires them to move their behaviors to be more in line with the group receiving recognition.

Other people won't adjust their behaviors unless there are consequences for not doing so. For them, consequences serve as a leverage point.

Another leverage point is money. People will often move their behaviors if the organization's incentive plan leads them to do so. For example, the C-Suite normally has an incentive compensation plan. Leaders know if they don't achieve certain goals, the incentive compensation plan will not open up for them.

Still, there is one leverage point that trumps all the others, and you'll notice it is at the top of Figure 15.9.

Values.

Simply put, people don't want to go against their values. Show values-driven people a better way of doing something—and present the evidence that it gets results—and their values will force them to do it.

Think about it. If you can prove to leaders that low turnover leads to fewer deaths, and you prove to them that rounding, for instance, reduces turnover, they will do the rounding. If they believe it will work, then values won't allow them *not* to do it.

The good news is that the vast majority of people in healthcare are already values-driven. They *want* to help people get well. They *want* to save lives. If they didn't, they wouldn't have chosen this profession. So if you can leverage their values, you've won half the battle.

And that's why connecting employees to "why" is such a powerful leadership technique. When they know the change they're being asked to make is not arbitrary, that its effectiveness is backed by hard evidence, they'll be more than happy to comply.

Get Specific.

A role of the leader is to help staff connect to "why." For example, a leader might connect the dots with patient financial services and registration staff by pointing out that because they do such a good job collecting co-pays, more money can be put back into the organization, which allows the organization as a whole to provide better patient care and better job security.

Or the leader might explain to the staff in BioMed that because they make sure the equipment is up to date and the proper preventative maintenance is completed, procedures can be done when they are supposed to be done, there are no delays, and they are performed to the highest clinical quality.

The leader might show a nurse that making a pre-visit phone call not only helps to reduce the number of patient no-shows, it may end up saving a patient's life by ensuring that her cancer is spotted early.

You can help employees connect to "why" through:

- Rounding conversations
- Storytelling opportunities (at employee forums or special events, for instance)
- Newsletter articles
- Thank-you notes

Great leaders look for every possible opportunity to remind employees of why what they do is meaningful.

Make It a Priority.

A physician who recently attended one of our two-day sessions literally cried. He told me that these two days had helped bring him back to why he got into healthcare in the first place. Yes, getting back in touch with the "why" can be a very powerful experience.

Studer Group recently conducted a survey asking employees when their supervisors last shared with them a note, a story, or an example of how an individual, a department, or the organization made a positive impact on the lives of others. Unfortunately, only 1 percent of the employees said they had heard a story of this nature in the last 90 days.

It is easy to get so caught up in running the operation that we miss opportunities to communicate to staff just how important the work they are doing is, not only to the organization, but to the patients.

When everyone in an organization is aligned in a common sense of purpose, we can survive the worst the external environment can throw at us.

Heal We/They Divisiveness.

The "we/they phenomenon" is what happens when one group or individual positions itself/himself/herself as different from others. It's the old "blame game." It usually happens in healthcare when a supervisor or leader is asked a difficult question and—rather than answering it directly—pins the blame on his or her boss or the C-Suite.

A tough external environment can be a breeding ground for we/they. It's not hard to understand why. When budgets are tight, people are more likely to be told "no"—*No, you can't have a pay increase…No, we can't hire any more support staff…No, the department can't have new equipment.*

Let's say a staff member asks a manager why the department can't buy a new copier. Instead of explaining that the hospital has other, more pressing priorities, the manager blames the tight-fisted people in Finance. That's we/they.

And here's another way we/they manifests. Remember the expectations gap we discussed in Chapter 1? When senior leaders understand the external environment better than their middle managers and supervisors, they may get frustrated and wonder why these groups aren't moving with a sense of urgency or figuring out creative solutions. "*We* are here working hard to save the organization…so why don't *they* see it?"

Or it could be that managers and supervisors are telling the staff they don't want these new guidelines senior leaders are forcing them to impose. "We are being micromanaged!" they may grumble. That, too, is we/they.

We/They Harms Organizations.

One thing's for sure: The we/they phenomenon widens the gap between the senior leaders and the rest of the organization. It is deeply destructive. It can cause an organization's flywheel—that self-perpetuating energy-

and-enthusiasm cycle that keeps employees striving for excellence—to grind to a halt.

Managers and employees who feel disenfranchised due to we/they certainly won't get behind vital changes you're trying to put in place. Oh, they may not openly sabotage your efforts, but neither will they put any energy and enthusiasm into them. We/they has robbed them of their sense of purpose and thrown a wet blanket over the passion that should be fueling their work.

So why do leaders perpetuate we/they—especially in times when the external environment calls upon everyone to do their best possible work?

Generally, we/they happens when a leader does not have the skill or the will to provide an answer that helps the staff member understand the "why." It's rarely malicious. Most leaders cause we/they divisiveness because they don't know how NOT to do so. It has been built into the culture for decades.

Communication Unites Organizational Cultures.

Fortunately, there are plenty of tools and techniques leaders can use to solve the problem. Many of them are touched on in this book. (The Tough Questions Exercise in Chapter 6 is one example.) You may already be doing some of them. The good news is that eliminating we/they is a function of communication—and improving communication automatically bridges the expectations gap.

And there is one more way to proactively heal we/they divisiveness: Practice the fine art of *managing up* and insist that all leaders do the same.

What is managing up? Basically, it's positioning other people, other departments, and the organization itself in the best possible light.

When an employee complains about his cut in health and vacation benefits, instead of blaming the CFO, a leader might say, "Mr. Rodriguez is doing a fantastic job of keeping our organization solvent in a very challenging economy. His leadership has made it possible for us to not only keep our doors open, but also to keep our team employed. I am very grateful for that!"

See the difference? We/they divides; managing up unites. And a united culture is far more likely to thrive in tough times.

A CLOSING THOUGHT

W orking in healthcare today provides many of the same rewards it has always provided. First and foremost, we get to save lives and make a difference—a calling most healthcare workers have in their DNA. This has not changed. What *has* changed? Just about everything else.

I know of no other industry in which payment systems are so diverse and the expectation is to provide high-quality service no matter what the payment. To do so, of course, means bearing the cost of recruiting and retaining talent, investing in state-of-the-art technology, and of course maintaining facilities that meet the most stringent codes.

Years ago I remember an article that compared being a leader in healthcare to driving a nitroglycerin truck. I could relate and I'll bet many of you can also. Today we are driving more than a truck; we are leading a convoy. The loads are much heavier, the road is steeper with sharper curves and more blind spots, and the surface is loaded with bumps, some natural and some self-imposed. No easy task on the best of days.

In any convoy, the alignment, actions, and accountability of each person are crucial. There must be clear outcomes and directions that are understood by all. The convoy must be led by leaders with proactive vision who know when to speed up, when to slow down, and when to stop and start again. There must be constant communication between all people so those following are safe and all adjustments are made consistently. Each driver must have the skill set to handle the journey. Because each person is dependent on those in front and in back, one mistake can put everyone at risk—and the closer one is to the front, the more responsibility that individual has to lead well.

Of course, in this case the load is not nitroglycerin but the future of healthcare.

Healthcare leadership is very difficult. I truly understand it is easier for someone like me to provide some results, gather the data to support the results, and tell others how to get them than to make it happen day in and day out 24 hours a day, 365 days a year. My job is the easy one.

The goal of this book is to assist readers in accessing their own ability and that of their fellow leaders and staff in completing the journey to make their organization the best. I have never met a leader in healthcare—or, for that fact, anyone in healthcare—who said his or her goal was to be average. This goal is not driven by ego but by the knowledge that being the best means people receive the best of care. It is the common language clearly understood by each person who works in healthcare.

The ability to adapt quickly to the ever-changing external environment is what will separate those who provide the best care from those who do not. This means alignment, action, and accountability that rest on the bedrock of healthcare, which is values.

I have found that when people see a way they can be better at their jobs, their values will not allow them not to implement their learnings.

Some years back my daughter took one of my grandchildren to a specialist due to some pain he seemed to be experiencing that just would not go away. The pain was not constant, but when it did come, it was hurtful and frightening to my grandson, his parents, and all who knew him. After tests were done, he was diagnosed with having a rare allergy to certain food ingredients.

My daughter called me on the way home from the specialist appointment. I could hear two very diverse tones in her voice. The first was relief they knew the answer and that the child's pain could be reduced and maybe even eliminated by a change in his diet. The other tone was a bit of remorse in that she had been providing him food that caused the pain. Intellectually, she was aware that she had not known the source of the problem—nor had anyone else—yet still she had feelings of remorse.

My first question is this: Was my daughter a bad mother prior to the doctor's appointment? I feel sure all will say no, she was not. She could not have been expected to know about the rare food allergy. I agree.

The next question is this: If she continued to provide food that contained ingredients that made the child ill, would that make her a bad mother? In this case, the answer would be yes.

Of course my daughter is a great mother and my grandson is doing well today. Her values as a mother would not allow her *not* to change her child's diet, no matter how difficult it was for him to give up foods he liked.

So no matter how difficult a needed change may be, it is values that keep us taking action toward the desired outcome. Those values that drive one to be a good partner, parent, and friend are the same values that drive our actions at work.

Values motivate us and keep us grounded. Once a person learns of a better way to do something, values will not allow him or her to be comfortable continuing on with the current method. Even though doing something a different way may be tough at first—it may be easier not to make a change—the internal discomfort is too great for people not to take the actions that lead to the best results for those they serve, those they serve with, and those they lead.

Making sure all people in the organization understand the challenges faced, that they have the skills to be successful in any environment, and that they're held accountable so the patient receives the best of care is values-driven leadership. My hope is that you have found the material in this book helpful in your journey to make healthcare a better place for patients to receive care, staff to work, and physicians to practice medicine. This brings us back to where we started: to have purpose, to do worthwhile work, and to make a difference.

Never underestimate the difference you have made and will continue to make. Thank you.

ORGANIZATIONAL

ASSESSMENT

T hank you for taking the time to read *Straight A Leadership*.

Right now you may be wondering: *How aligned is my organization in its perception of the external environment? Are we training leaders properly and holding them accountable for results? How consistent is our leadership—and how effective are we at standardizing best practices and implementing them throughout the organization?*

Studer Group would like to help you discover the answers. Here's how:

1. Log onto www.studergroup.com/StraightALeadership.

2. Enter your name and contact information and we'll contact you regarding how your organization can take the same organizational assessment you have just read about.

We believe that good organizations always want to be better—and getting a true picture of where you stand right now is the best way to move forward on the journey.

RESOURCES

Accelerate the momentum of your Healthcare Flywheel®.

Access additional resources at www.studergroup.com/ StraightALeadership.

STUDER GROUP COACHING:

Organizational Coaching Line

Studer Group® coaches hospitals and healthcare systems providing detailed framework and practical how-tos that create change. Studer Group coaches work side-by-side establishing, accelerating, and hardwiring the necessary changes to create a culture of excellence. In our work, Studer Group has identified a core of three critical elements that must be in place for great organizational performance once a commitment is made to the pillar approach to goal setting and the Nine Principles® of Behavior.

Emergency Department Coaching Line

Is a comprehensive approach to improving service and operational efficiency in the Emergency Department. Our team of ED coach experts will partner with you to implement best practices, proven tools, and tactics using our Evidence-Based Leadership^{SM} approach to improve results in all five pillars—People, Service, Quality, Finance, and Growth. Key deliverables include decreasing staff turnover, improving employee, physician, and patient satisfaction, decreasing door-to-doctor times, reducing left without being seen rates, increasing upfront cash collections, and increasing patient volumes and revenue.

Disruptive Behavior Coaching Line

Research suggests that nearly three out of four healthcare providers have experienced some type of disruptive or intimidating behavior in the course of their work. Studer Group has partnered with the Center for Patient and Professional Advocacy at Vanderbilt University Medical Center to help healthcare organizations address this issue. Comprehensive on-site coaching, assessment, gap analysis, facilitation, leadership training, and speaking are available for audiences including boards, senior leaders, physicians, and managers.

To learn more about Studer Group coaching, visit www.studergroup.com.

BOOKS: categorized by audience

Senior Leaders & Physicians

Leadership and Medicine—A book that makes sense of the complex challenges of healthcare and offers a wealth of practical advice to future generations, written by Floyd D. Loop, MD, former chief executive of the Cleveland Clinic (1989-2004).

Engaging Physicians: A Manual to Physician Partnership—A tactical and passionate roadmap for physician collaboration to generate organizational high performance, written by Stephen C. Beeson, MD.

Physicians

Practicing Excellence: A Physician's Manual to Exceptional Health Care—This book, written by Stephen C. Beeson, MD, is a brilliant guide to implementing physician leadership and behaviors that will create a high-performance workplace.

All Leaders

Hardwiring Excellence—A *BusinessWeek* bestseller, this book is a road map to creating and sustaining a "Culture of Service and Operational Excellence" that drives bottom-line results.
Written by Quint Studer

Results That Last—A Wall Street Journal bestseller by Quint Studer that teaches leaders in every industry how to apply his tactics and strategies to their own organizations to build a corporate culture that consistently reaches and exceeds its goals.

Hardwiring Flow: Systems and Processes for Seamless Patient Care—Drs. Thom Mayer and Kirk Jensen delve into one of the most critical issues facing healthcare leaders today: patient flow.

Eat That Cookie!: Make Workplace Positivity Pay Off... For Individuals, Teams, and Organizations—Written by Liz Jazwiec, RN, this book is funny, inspiring, relatable, and is packed with realistic, down-to-earth tactics to infuse positivity into your culture.

"I'm Sorry to Hear That..." Real Life Responses to Patients' 101 Most Common Complaints About Health Care— When you respond to a patient's complaint, you are responding to the patient's sense of helplessness and anxiety. The service recovery scripts offered in this book can help you recover a patient's confidence in you and your organization. Authored by Susan Keane Baker and Leslie Bank.

What's Right in Health Care: 365 Stories of Purpose, Worthwhile Work, and Making a Difference—A collaborative effort of stories from healthcare professionals across the nation. This 742-page book shares a story a day submitted by your friends and colleagues. It is a daily reminder about why we answered this calling and why we stay with it—to serve a purpose, to do worthwhile work, and to make a difference.

101 Answers to Questions Leaders Ask—By Quint Studer and Studer Group coaches, offers practical, prescriptive solutions to some of the many questions he's received from healthcare leaders around the country.

Nurse Leaders and Nurses

The Nurse Leader Handbook: The Art and Science of Nurse Leadership—By Studer Group senior nursing and physician leaders from across the country, is filled with knowledge that provides nurse leaders with a solid foundation for success. It also serves as a reference they can revisit again and again when they have questions or need a quick refresher course in a particular area of the job.

Inspired Nurse and Inspired Journal—By Rich Bluni, RN, helps maintain and recapture the inspiration nurses felt at the start of their journey with action-oriented "spiritual stretches" and stories that illuminate those sacred moments we all experience.

Emergency Department Team

Excellence in the Emergency Department—A book by Stephanie Baker, RN, CEN, MBA, is filled with proven, easy-to-implement, step-by-step instructions that will help you move your Emergency Department forward.

For more information about books and other resources, visit www.firestarterpublishing.com.

MAGAZINES:

Hardwired Results - Issue 11, 2009
Tools to create accountability and add dollars to your bottom line

Hardwired Results - Issue 12, 2009
Offers a wealth of evidence-backed insights on addressing the three "As"—Alignment, Action, Accountability—to achieve peak performance.

Visit www.studergroup.com to view additional *Hardwiring Results* magazines.

ARTICLES:

Keep Your Patients Coming Back
MGMA Connexion
August 2008

Quint Studer on 5 Important Issues Facing Healthcare Leaders
The Hospital Review
November 14, 2008

Unlocking the FEAR Foothold
Quint Studer
March 2009

Evidence-Based Leadership
Projects@Work
Quint Studer

How to Achieve and Sustain Excellence
Healthcare Financial Management

To read these articles and view other resources, please visit www.studergroup.com/StraightALeadership.

SOFTWARE SOLUTIONS:

Leader Evaluation Manager™: Results Through Focus and Accountability

Studer Group's Leader Evaluation Manager is a web-based application that automates the goal setting and performance review process for all leaders, while ensuring that the performance metrics of individual leaders are aligned with the overall goals of the organization. By using Leader Evaluation Manager, both leaders and their supervisors will clearly understand from the beginning of the year what goals need to be accomplished to achieve a successful annual review, can plan quarterly tasks with completion targets under each goal, and view monthly report cards to manage progress.

To learn more, please visit www.firestarterpublishing. com.

INSTITUTES:

Taking You and Your Organization to the Next Level

Learn the tools, tactics, and strategies that are needed to Take You and Your Organization to the Next Level at this two-day institute. You will walk away with your passion ignited, and with Evidence-Based Leadership℠ strategies to create a sustainable culture of excellence.

Nuts and Bolts of Operational Excellence in the Emergency Department

Improve patient flow and build service and operational excellence in your Emergency Department as Studer Group experts with extensive and ongoing real-life ED experience share proven tactics to improve Emergency Department outcomes.

What's Right in Health Care^{SM}

One of the largest healthcare peer-to-peer learning conferences in the nation, *What's Right in Health Care* brings organizations together to share ideas that have been proven to make healthcare better.

To review a listing of Studer Group institutes or to register for an institute, visit www.studergroup.com/institutes.

For information on Continuing Education Credits, visit www.studergroup.com/cmecredits.

Visit www.studergroup.com/StraightALeadership to access and download many of the resources, examples, and tools mentioned in *Straight A Leadership*.

ABOUT THE AUTHOR

Quint Studer is founder and CEO of Studer Group®, a coaching company that implements evidence-based leadership systems and practices that help organizations attain and sustain outstanding results. He spends much of his time creating, harvesting, and sharing best practices from his company's "national learning lab" of hundreds of organizations and thousands of leaders.

Studer Group is known for providing and teaching how to implement practical, research-based tools and techniques for better operational performance. Organizations experience excellence in service, quality, finance, people, and growth.

A frequent keynoter at national trade, professional association, and organization meetings, Studer meets with more than 1,200 healthcare leaders monthly at client engagements and Studer Group-sponsored institutes. He also is a frequently interviewed healthcare leader in national media. While this is good, he prefers to spend his time in organizations learning.

Inc. magazine named Studer its Master of Business, making him the only healthcare leader to have ever won this award. Twice *Modern Healthcare* has chosen Quint as one of the 100 Most Powerful People in Healthcare.

In addition to *Straight A Leadership*, Studer has written two bestselling books. His first, *BusinessWeek* bestseller *Hardwiring Excellence*, is one of the bestselling leadership books ever written for healthcare. More than 350,000 copies have been sold. His second book, *Results That Last*, hit the *Wall Street Journal's* bestseller list of business books.

How to Order Additional Copies of

Straight A Leadership
Alignment, Action, Accountability

Orders may be placed:

Online at:
www.firestarterpublishing.com
www.studergroup.com

By phone at: 866-354-3473

By mail at: Fire Starter Publishing
913 Gulf Breeze Parkway, Suite 6
Gulf Breeze, FL 32561

(Bulk discounts are available.)

Straight A Leadership
is also available online at www.amazon.com.